Opera Guide

17

The Marriage of Figaro
Le Nozze di Figaro

Mozart

Nancy Storace, the English soprano who created the role of Susanna in Vienna, 1786 (Raymond Mander and Joe Mitchenson Theatre Collection)

Preface

This series, published under the auspices of English National Opera and The Royal Opera, aims to prepare audiences to enjoy and evaluate opera performances. Each book contains the complete text, set out in the original language together with a current performing translation. The accompanying essays have been commissioned as general introductions to aspects of interest in each work. As many illustrations and musical examples as possible have been included because the sound and spectacle of opera are clearly central to any sympathetic appreciation of it. We hope that, as companions to the opera should be, they are well-informed, witty and attractive.

Nicholas John
Series Editor

17

The Marriage of Figaro
Le Nozze di Figaro

Wolfgang Amadeus Mozart

Opera Guide Series Editor: Nicholas John

Published in association with
English National Opera

Calder Publications · London
Riverrun Press · New York

First published in Great Britain, 1983, by
John Calder (Publishers) Ltd, London

This edition published in Great Britain, 1996, by
Calder Publications Limited
179 Kings Cross Road, London WC1X 9BZ

and

First published in the U.S.A., 1983, by
Riverrun Press Inc.
1170 Broadway
New York, NY 10001

Second impression 1989

Third impression 1996

BRITISH LIBRARY CATALOGUING IN PUBLICATION DATA

Mozart, Wolfgang Amadeus
  Le nozze di Figaro = The Marriage of Figaro.–(Opera guides;17)
  1. Mozart, Wolfgang Amadeus. Nozze di Figaro
  2. Operas–Librettos
  I. Title   II. da Ponte, Lorenzo
  III. John, Nicholas   IV. Series
  782.1'2   ML50.M939

ISBN 0-7145-3771-3

LIBRARY OF CONGRESS CATALOGING IN PUBLICATION DATA is available

Typeset in Plantin by Maggie Spooner Typesetting, London.
Pre-press by On-Line Colour, New York.
Printed in the U.S.A. by Rose Printing, Tallahassee, Florida.

Contents

List of Illustrations

A Society Marriage

John Wells

According to Beaumarchais, its original author, *The Marriage of Figaro* was written at the request of that pillar of the Ancien Régime, the Prince de Conti, Commander-in-Chief of the Army under Louis XV. According to Napoleon, it was part of the mechanism of the Revolution, a central cog already *cog* beginning to turn as early as six o'clock in the evening of Tuesday, April 27, 1784, when the play received its first public performance in Paris at the Comédie Française.

Both statements are probably true, and for anyone interested in the mysterious interaction between art and politics, it would be hard to find a more fascinating story: Beaumarchais, watchmaker to Madame de Pompadour, secret agent to Louis XVI, creating a piece of dramatic machinery credited with *commissione* the destruction of the society that commissioned it, only to be turned, by Mozart and da Ponte, into a work of art in which we recognise the most perfect flowering of the civilisation it is alleged to have destroyed.

Pierre-Auguste Caron de Beaumarchais had been born plain Caron in 1732, the son of a watchmaker in the rue St Denis. His first revolutionary act, at the age of twenty-one, was to invent a new kind of escapement, enabling him to make a watch that was not only accurate to the second, but also small enough to fit inside a ring, and this he presented to Madame de Pompadour. The Court watchmaker, Lepaute, claimed that he had invented it first, but Caron protested to the Academy of Sciences, won his case, and took over Lepaute's Royal Patent.

He strengthened his position at Versailles by marrying an influential but, as he discovered on her death a year later, penniless widow, from whose estate in the country however he took the title de Beaumarchais, adopting the very suitable motto *'Ma Vie est un Combat'*. By the age of twenty-seven he had further established himself with characteristic versatility as music master to the daughters of Louis XV, and taught them his favourite instrument, the harp. From this followed various well-paid Court appointments, including the administration of hunting rights, which required him to spend a considerable amount of time in the law-courts, passing judgement on poaching offences. He also formed lucrative associations with some of the leading financiers of the day.

In 1764 he made a journey to Madrid, combining the discreet advancement of French business interests in the newly-acquired Spanish colony of Louisiana with the official purpose of his visit, which was to straighten out a breach of promise case between his elder sister, Lisette, who was then thirty-nine, and a Spanish journalist called Clavijo. Beaumarchais's own account of the two men's meeting, his arriving incognito, fascinating his adversary with a tale of faithless love, and then, in a final *coup de théâtre*, revealing himself as the brother of the abandoned woman, was subsequently to provide Goethe with the plot of his drama *Clavigo*.

Beaumarchais's own first excursion into the theatre, *Eugénie*, was written in 1767, when he was thirty-five. It was in the style of uplifting middle-class realism advocated by Diderot, known as the *drame bourgeois*, and was given a mixed reception. His second, *Les Deux Amis, ou le Négociant de Lyon*, was

John Tomlinson as Figaro in Jonathan Miller's 1978 ENO production (photo: Anthony Crickmay)

written three years later and failed entirely. But he had also been writing comedy, in the form of what were called *parades*; coarse, knockabout sketches, performed privately, 'in the flickering shadows of the drawing-room', popular in fashionable society, but based on the rough street-theatre of the Paris Fairs. He had also seen similar shows in Madrid, known as *entremeses*, which incorporated the Barber as a stock comic character.

Life too was providing him with some rich material. He had married again, this time to a widow with money, who had died two years later. He had also come into an inheritance, left him by one of his financiers, Pâris-Duvernay, which he successfully defended against rival claimants. In 1773, at the age of 41, he became involved in a farcical quarrel over a certain Mlle Ménard, which was to leave him bankrupt, in disgrace, but with a lasting and genuine hatred of hereditary privilege, and also, by a skilful use of journalism and stage-management, with the public reputation of a revolutionary hero struggling against oppression.

His opponent was the Marquis de Chaulnes, a grotesquely fat and violently irascible man who went about with a monkey on a chain. Until then, he and Beaumarchais had been the best of friends: now Chaulnes threatened to kill him, dragged him from the Bench where he was trying a poaching case, ripped the wigs from the heads of anyone who tried to interfere, snatched a pen out of

Beaumarchais's hand and threw it out of the window, scratched his face and stabbed his servant through the hand with a fork. As a result they were both imprisoned.

Hearing that the magistrate was to be a notoriously corrupt individual by the name of Goëzman, Beaumarchais sent his wife a jewelled watch and a hundred louis to ease the wheels of justie. Madame Goëzman accepted the present, and asked for a further fifteen louis for the clerk. How much Chaulnes gave her is not on record, but Beaumarchais lost the case, was ordered to pay costs, and a crushing fine which reduced him to penury. Madame Goëzman, very decently, returned the hundred louis and the watch, but kept the fifteen louis she had demanded for the clerk. Having made it his motto that life was a battle, Beaumarchais counterattacked. Without a penny to his name and his seventy-five year old father turned out into the street, he launched a series of pamphlets, the *Memorials against Goëzman*, admitting the entire truth and demanding the return of his fifteen louis. Goëzman was dismissed, Beaumarchais publicly disgraced and deprived of his rights as a citizen.

Mysteriously, Louis XVI retained his services as a secret agent, and during his ensuing exile in London he continued to work for Versailles, rooting out and suppressing the publishers of Anti-Royalist French pamphlets. He also, lest farce be forgotten entirely, lent assistance to another French agent, the Chevalier d'Eon, a transvestite of vigorously heterosexual leanings who was to be seen lifting his dress in the drawing-rooms of fashionable London society to expose his battle scars, and was believed by some to be the father of George IV. Beaumarchais negotiated a pension for him from the King of France with which he bought a wardrobe of expensive dresses for the Chevalier's return to Versailles; there was general disappointment when he arrived there dressed as a Dragoon, only reverting to a frock for his second day at Court.

Before embarking on his next adventurous career, running guns to General Washington, which also cost him a fortune since the American Revolutionaries presumably saw no cause to pay once French 'military advisers' became official allies, Beaumarchais returned to France in 1775 for the first performance of *The Barber of Seville*. It opened on a Friday and was booed off by the first night audience.

'Seeing the enemy relentless', he writes in his mock-pompous defence of the play in a preface to the first edition, 'the pit restless, rough and roaring aloud like the waves of the sea, and all too well aware that grumbling thunder of that kind can herald storms that have brought about the wreck of more than one proud enterprise, I fell to thinking that many plays in five acts (like my own), although excellently made in every particular (like my own), would not have foundered lock, stock and barrel (like my own), if the author had taken a bold decision (like my own). *The God of the Cabal is angry!* I cried aloud to the actors: *Children! We needs must make some sacrifice.* Then, giving the devil his due and ripping my manuscript apart: *God of the hissers, booers and disturbers of the peace,* I roared, *Must you have blood? Then take Act Four and may your fury be appeased!*' After a week-end of cutting and re-staging the show re-opened and was immediately a success. 'Poor Figaro, who had been unmercifully thrashed to the monotonous chanting of the Cabal, and almost buried on Friday . . . rose again on Sunday with a vigour that the rigours of a long Lent and the fatigue of twenty-seven public performances have not yet sapped. But who knows how long it can go on? Not more than five or six hundred years at the very most, I should have said, in a country as fickle and unpredictable as France!'

Whether or not Beaumarchais realised that he had written a play that would survive his own century, he must have recognised that in his Andalusian

Marie Roze Perkins (left) and Zaré Thalberg (right) as Cherubino (Theatre Museum)

barber he, and the liberal-minded majority of the theatre-going public, had found a mouthpiece. Frédéric Grendel* has argued very plausibly that Figaro *was* Beaumarchais, *Fils* — pronounced in the 18th century *Fi — Caron*, and that all the autobiographical details, particularly during the long monologue in the original *Marriage of Figaro*, tally exactly with the events in the author's life. Certainly the figure of the barber with his razor resting against the Count's Adam's apple is a powerful image of the vigorous middle class confronting hereditary privilege.

It is in the same preface to *The Barber of Seville* that Beaumarchais imagines what might happen after the curtain comes down: Bartholo and Figaro are still arguing about money, and begin hitting each other. In the course of the brawl that follows, the old Doctor is punching Figaro's head when he sees the mark of a hot spatula and stops to cry out in delight: Figaro is his long-lost son, stolen away by gipsies. Marceline is his mother. 'What an end to the play! What an Act Six! Better than any tragedy at the Théâtre Français! But enough of that . . .'

This is the story, Beaumarchais claims in his preface to *The Marriage of Figaro*, that the Prince de Conti challenged him to make into a sequel. What the public, and what Beaumarchais wanted, was more Figaro. The main plot, he explains in the second preface, is extremely simple: 'a Spanish Grandee, in love with a girl he intends to seduce, and her efforts, those of her future husband and the Grandee's wife to frustrate him in a design that his position in society, his wealth and his dissolute character make him entirely capable of accomplishing.'

By the time Mozart and da Ponte began work on the opera in Vienna in 1785, the play had already caused an uproar in Paris, and Joseph II, the Austrian Emperor, had banned a version that was to have been performed

* *Beaumarchais, The Man who was Figaro* Tr. Roger Graves, Macdonald and Jane's 1977.

there. Da Ponte therefore set about reducing its overtly political content to a minimum, cutting a great deal of Figaro's verbal skirmishing with the Count, and the whole of his long tirade against privilege as he waits under the chestnut trees — da Ponte transformed them into pine trees, perhaps in some fit of Italianate yearning for the North — for the feudal lord he believes is about to plunder his 'property' in the person of Suzanne. Marceline's speech in defence of women's rights, on the other hand, which follows her reconciliation with Figaro and the Doctor, and which had been suppressed in Paris by the actors themselves, was partially retained by da Ponte in Marcellina's aria in Act Four, though it is not always performed.

But even with Figaro's closing couplet of the *vaudeville*, the song and dance that brings the stage play to an end, in which he compares the mortality of kings to the immortal glory awaiting Voltaire, it is difficult to imagine the play creating more than a frisson of drawing room egalitarianism in the extravagantly-dressed stars of Parisian high society who crammed the new auditorium of the Comédie Française — 'that mine of white icing sugar' — for the five hours of cheering and rapturous applause that marked the first performance. The play did literally bring about the death of three enthusiastic theatre-goers, crushed by the crowd of five thousand that besieged the theatre from eight o'clock in the morning, and poured in when the gates were opened at twelve noon, six hours before the curtain was due to rise. According to one account, their dead bodies were held upright by the weight of numbers, and appeared to be listening to the play. But it was predominantly an aristocratic audience, three hundred of whom thought it was the greatest privilege to be allowed to eat a picnic in the actors' dressing rooms. The artistic event of the century, perhaps, but not, on the face of it, a great political turning point.

The answer to the riddle is to be found in the mainspring of the plot. The Count, having renounced the *Droit de Seigneur*, his absolute power over his subjects, is trying illicitly to re-establish it. Louis XVI, vacillating over the liberal reforms that Beaumarchais believed would lead to Constitutional

An early (1800) piano score of the opera (Royal College of Music)

Catherine Stephens as Susanna at Covent Garden in 1819 (Raymond Mander and Joe Mitchenson Theatre Collection)

Monarchy, behaved in exactly the same way. When Beaumarchais gave him the manuscript to read in 1782, he said it would be necessary to demolish the Bastille before the play could be performed in public without embarrassing the Government. Combative as ever, Beaumarchais organised a series of private readings that became the rage of Paris, and the King in response to pressure at Court gave his permission for a private performance at Versailles in the summer of 1783. Beaumarchais rehearsed it for four weeks, and three hours before the curtain was to go up the King cancelled it. Rage and despair on the part of the audience, wild talk of tyranny and oppression.

By September of the same year the King had changed his mind again, and allowed a single performance at Grennevilliers, the country house of the Comte de Vandreuil. Marie Antoinette was to have been present, but at the last minute sent apologies and said she was unwell. Gaining fresh momentum from this success, the publicity campaign continued. Beaumarchais called a semi-public meeting with the six official censors, arguing through the play line by line, delighting privileged spectators with his wit and skilfully incorporating their more amusing suggestions in the text: Madame de Matignon was credited with inventing the colour of Chérubin's ribbon. Permission was granted, and after a two-year build-up, the comedy scored what was probably the most spectacular success of any opening night in history.

A few days later, as if that triumph was not enough, Beaumarchais tested the weakness of the Government to even more excruciatingly absurd limits. Irritated by an attack from Suard, the Chief of Police, he said that when he had done battle with lions and tigers he couldn't be bothered with repulsive little insects that only dared to bite under cover of darkness. Not wishing to be listed among the big cats vanquished by the lion-tamer, Louis XVI, after customary

Maggie Teyte who sang Cherubino at Sir Thomas Beecham's Mozart festival at His Majesty's Theatre in 1910 (Royal Opera House Archives)

13

hesitation, scribbled an order for his arrest on the seven of spades during a game of cards, and Beaumarchais was imprisoned. Instead of the Bastille, reserved for respectable political opponents, he was confined in St Lazare, a leper hospital and the gaol for prostitutes and petty thieves.

A gigantic sum was raised by his friends for bail, intercession was made at Versailles, and the King wrote an order for his immediate release. Beaumarchais ignored it. He would not leave the prison until he had an assurance that the entire Cabinet would attend *The Marriage of Figaro* 'as a gesture of respect for the author'. Incredibly, they did so, rising to their feet at the end of the performance and applauding him. By way of making additional amends, the King also organised a gala performance of *The Barber of Seville* at Versailles, with Marie Antoinette playing Rosine.

Many of those who metaphorically lost their heads at the first night of *The Marriage of Figaro* died on the guillotine. Beaumarchais was exiled, once again for gun-running, and remained abroad until 1796, when he returned, still clinging to his title, as Citizen Caron de Beaumarchais, describing it as his *nom de guerre*. He had continued to promote extravagant schemes, including a complete edition of the works of Voltaire with lottery prizes for those lucky enough to buy certain numbered copies, and a gigantic monument to Liberty on the site now occupied by the Eiffel Tower. At the height of the Terror he had been working on the third and last of the Figaro plays, *A Mother's Guilt*: this time it is set in the present. Aguas Frescas has been sold up, the Count, now plain Monsieur Almaviva, is living in Paris. The comedy is over, and the pigeons have come home to roost. Chérubin, having given the Countess an illegitimate child, has died in despair on the battlefield, Almaviva has brought his daughter by another woman to live in the house as his ward, their only legitimate child has been shot dead in a duel, and the family is being preyed upon by a villainous Irish adventurer, Captain Bégearss, inevitably based on yet another personal enemy of Beaumarchais, a lawyer called Bergasse. It is left to Figaro and Suzanne, now grown old in service, to unmask and expel the interloper.

The play, which had met with a luke-warm reception before his exile, was revived with great success on his return, and Napoleon claimed that it was his favourite work. After months spent studying the possibilities of aviation, a chance, he felt, that had been missed, 'that could have changed the face of the earth more radically than the invention of the compass', Beaumarchais died in his sleep, probably of apoplexy, in the spring of 1799. His energy and fighting spirit survive in his greatest work, *The Marriage of Figaro*: still sufficiently alarming to authority, for all the ambiguity of its political origins, to have been banned at the Comédie Française throughout the German Occupation.

Mirella Freni who first sang Susanna at Covent Garden in 1963 (Royal Opera House Archives)

Rita Hunter as Marcellina and Noel Mangin as Dr Bartolo in the 1965 Sadler's Wells production (photo: Reg Wilson)

Elizabeth Harwood as Susanna and Raimund Herincx as the Count in the 1965 Sadler's Wells production (photo: Reg Wilson)

Alexander Oliver, Heather Begg, Victor Braun and Noel Mangin at Covent Garden in 1977 (photo: Reg Wilson)

A Musical Commentary

Basil Deane

'Dramma per musica' — drama through music: the oldest, and still the best, definition of opera. And the character of any opera will be determined by the manner in which the librettist and composer resolve the inherent tension between these two elements. For tension there must be. There are many types of drama; but all involve individuals in specific circumstances interacting and reacting to outside events, in a recognisably human time-scale. Music is an unspecific art, and it functions within its own structures and its own time-scale. It must be integrated with the drama in a way that illuminates the characters and articulates the action, without losing its unique expressive power. The history of opera is the history of attempted solutions to this problem.

By the 18th century Italian opera has assumed two fairly stylised forms. *Opera seria* dealt with important personages participating in grand historical or mythological events. These individuals expressed themselves in a series of arias projecting their current emotional state. And here arises at its most acute the problem of dramatic and musical reconciliation. An unbroken succession of soliloquies is not after all the customary mode of human communication. The problem is compounded by the structure of the aria. It is in ternary, or ABA, form. The return of the first section brings the music back to the home key and allows the singer to embellish the original melody. However desirable musically, in terms of advancing the action this procedure is inherently undramatic since the composer also returns to the original text. The return of

Left: Zélie de Lussan and right: Lillian Nordica as Cherubino (Stuart-Liff Collection)

17

the first section, necessary for musical reasons, is, in terms of advancing the action, inherently undramatic. The best composers were of course aware of the difficulty, and the approach by a composer such as Handel to the aria is of the greatest interest. But in the hands of lesser figures *opera seria* became a series of staged concert arias, in which the dramatic structure was irrelevant or virtually absent.

The alternative form, *opera buffa*, was not so stereotyped. In the comic operas of Cimarosa and Paisiello, for example, the characters, drawn from less exalted stations, often had a liveliness and a naturalness missing in *opera seria*. Musical numbers were shorter, and simple ensembles played a more prominent part. The action moved forward more rapidly. But the fairly restricted musical idioms allowed for little depth of character portrayal. Nevertheless it was this tradition which, however modestly, provided the foundation for Mozart's great *opera buffa*.

Beaumarchais's play, it is well recognized, is in several senses revolutionary. So, too, in dramatic terms, is da Ponte's libretto. It stands head and shoulders above all the earlier *opera buffa* librettos by virtue of its length, its combination of clarity and complexity, its consistency, its momentum. But perhaps the most revolutionary thing about it is its use of ensembles. Of its twenty-eight numbers, only half are for solo voice. Such a concentration on ensembles was unprecedented in 18th-century opera. It brought a new dramatic and psychological realism to the medium. Instead of taking characters and their emotions at their own word, so to speak, audiences could now see and evaluate them in a variety of social contexts. This above all was the great opportunity that da Ponte's libretto offered to Mozart — the opportunity of presenting fully-rounded characters in a range of evolving situations. The composer understood this, and by musical genius transformed the already brilliant concept of da Ponte into one of the great masterpieces of dramatic art.

He was, in compositional terms, extremely well equipped to do so. The classical style reached maturity in the 1780s. The symphony, concerto and sonata offered flexible, coherent forms, based on the integration of contrasting musical ideas, both small and large scale. The composition of the orchestra became standardised and the combination of strings, wind and percussion offered a wide potential of textures and instrumental colours. By the time he came to write *Figaro* Mozart was already a master of this new, exciting language; indeed he himself had already made a major contribution to its rapid and continuing evolution. The Overture is itself a fine illustration of his superb accomplishment as an instrumental composer. It is based on three main themes [1, 2, 3]. All his fingerprints are manifest; brilliant tuttis, singing melodies, imaginative orchestration, rhythmic drive, subtly varied harmonies. Its powerful drive and its elegance and carefully calculated detail belie the haste in which it was written, a matter of hours before the first performance.

The Overture ends, the curtain rises, and Figaro and Susanna are together, Figaro measuring the room they have been allocated, and Susanna trying on her wedding hat. The orchestral introduction epitomises Mozart's approach to musical characterisation. The passage contains two contrasting themes, one robust, the other insinuating [4, 5]. In the duet Figaro is associated with the first, Susanna with the second. Susanna is gently insistent that she should have Figaro's undivided attention, and he eventually abandons his measurements, and his theme, joining her in harmonious tenths. Not only are the personalities of the two protagonists outlined; Susanna's capacity for leading her betrothed is established as is also the warmth in their relationship.

The following duet tells us more about them. Figaro has taken the Count's

Hermann Prey as Figaro and Teresa Stratas as Susanna at Covent Garden in 1977 (photo: Christina Burton)

gift of this convenient room at face value; Susanna is much more attuned to her employer's real motives. This time they both use a variant of the same theme [6]. But the tone of Susanna's ironical answer to Figaro is deliciously established by a pre-emptive switch to the minor key. Figaro is not stupid. He takes Susanna's point, and again the duet ends in unity.

Up until now, Susanna has made the running. Now Figaro, seeing the situation clearly for the first time, asserts himself. Mozart chooses the framework of a courtly minuet, no doubt with the Count in mind [7]. But as the music progresses, the symbolic sounds of the horns, doubled by *pizzicato* strings, and the sudden leaps in the vocal part, as well as the stabbing accents, convey Figaro's anger, which breaks the conventional surface in the *Presto* outburst [8]. Figaro aroused is to be reckoned with.

Bartolo and Marcellina now arrive. Middle-aged and worldly, they form a contrast to the young lovers. Here for the first time in the opera Mozart draws

Dennis Wicks as Bartolo and Ava June as Marcellina in the ENO production, 1978 (photo: Anthony Crickmay)

on the resources of *opera seria*. Among the categories of aria employed in *opera seria* was the 'rage' aria. Bartolo gives vent to his delight at the prospect of revenge on Figaro in a parodied example of the type, full of unison passages, accompanied by the pomp of horns, trumpets and drums [9]. The quick 'patter' passage in the middle belongs however to the *buffa* world [10].

The women's relationship is no less antagonistic, but socially concealed. In the following duet an exchange of compliments turns quickly into one of insults, in which Susanna has all the natural advantages. The exchange is repeated, and here occurs an example of the conflict between musical and dramatic exigencies. Dramatically the repetition of the text is most implausible; since Marcellina has been deeply insulted and bested, she is very unlikely to go through the same situation again. But, although Mozart describes this number (as he did the earlier ones) as a duettino, to end after the first exchange would have been musically too sudden. So here, as in other similar situations, the resolution in stage terms depends ultimately on the skill of the producer and his singers.

Cherubino now enters. In Beaumarchais's time the emotional development and sexual education of adolescents was of fashionable interest in French aristocratic circles. Cherubino, the Countess's page, is in the tradition. He is still in the initial stages of discovery and self-awareness, in love with love. His longings are diffuse, his affections transferable. His aria, with its breathless phrases, its palpitating accompaniment, its hesitant chromaticisms, evokes the excitement of his emotions [11].

So far the Count has been an unseen but potentially threatening influence on events. With his appearance the action quickens. Cherubino, fearful of his wrath, hides. The Count resumes his attempted seduction of Susanna, but, on

20

Basilio's arrival, he too conceals himself. The stage is set for a classic piece of situation comedy. Basilio's insinuations about the page's relationship with the Countess bring the infuriated husband out of hiding. The terzetto that follows provides Mozart with his first opportunity in the opera for building a large-scale musical structure, and dramatic and musical content are mutually dependent. The emotions of the three characters are embodied in the opening material: the Count's rage, momentarily contained, then given full vent [12]; Basilio's silky obsequiousness [13a]; Susanna's apprehension [13b]. These three elements provide much of the subsequent musical material. When the music moves from B flat to its second key of F, there is a momentary lull as both men hasten to support Susanna when she pretends to faint. But her perception of the danger of revealing Cherubino, and her quick reaction, hurry the action and the music onward. Basilio smoothly reintroduces the subject of the page again, and, as the Count resumes his initial threats, so too the opening material returns, now varied, re-ordered and expanded to encompass the discovery of Cherubino. Perfectly illustrative of the developing action, the terzetto, 220 bars long, is in fact a fully-fledged movement in sonata form.

The chorus of peasants, led by Figaro, praising the Count, has in itself a charming folk-like simplicity. In the context of Figaro's new attitude to his master, and of the immediately preceding events, its dramatic purport, is, of course, ironical.

To begin an *opera buffa* with a duet is in itself unusual; to end an act with a solo is more so. Convention dictated that this was the place for an ensemble. But no exit could be more effective than that of Cherubino, departing reluctantly for the wars. Figaro's aria became an instant 'hit' when the opera was performed in Prague, and it has remained one ever since. As so often, a straightforward exterior conceals great art. Those who know the aria well (and who does not?) should observe the detail of the orchestral accompaniment [15]; the contrasting textures; the woodwind and string embellishments; the sparing use of trumpets and drums until Cherubino sets out for victory and glory in a blaze of fanfares [16].

The discovery of Cherubino in the 1965 Sadler's Wells production with Margaret Neville as Cherubino (photo: Reg Wilson)

21

One principal figure has still to be introduced: the Countess. She has a dignity and restraint appropriate to her position, yet she is also a loving wife, deeply wounded by her husband's behaviour. A *seria* rather than a *buffa* character, she makes her entrance fittingly at the beginning of Act Two with a solo number, in which she implores the gods to revive her husband's love. Mozart eschews the fully-fledged aria. Instead he writes a *cavatina* — a single section composition in which she retains her outward poise; the melodic line is chaste and tender, and moves above a simple but firm bass line [17]. But her inner agitation is conveyed by the gently throbbing accompaniment figure, with its poignant chromatic inflections. This textural combination is not uncommon in Mozart's mature slow movements, as, for example, in the string quartet in E flat major, K. 428. Nowhere is it more dramatically effective than here. The characterisation is enhanced by the first use in the opera of a pair of clarinets as obligato instruments, moving in melting euphony.

In the second scene of the Act, which takes place in recitative, Figaro expounds to the two women his plot to confuse and ensnare the Count, by arousing the latter's suspicions about his wife's fidelity. The Countess, understandably, is hesitant; but she is won over by the lovers, and Figaro reaffirms his intention of making the Count dance to his tune. Cherubino, who has contrived to delay his depature, joins the women, and is easily persuaded to sing the song he has composed for the Countess [18]. Its blend of youthful hope and uncertainty is irresistible. In preparation for the intrigue against the Count, Susanna makes Cherubino try on a dress, and sings a cheerful, busy

Lillian Watson as Susanna and Valerie Masterson as the Countess in Jonathan Miller's 1978 ENO production, designed by Patrick Robertson and Rosemary Vercoe (photo: Anthony Crickmay)

aria while she fits him out [19]. The scene projects a subtle blend of comedy and underlying eroticism, and the Countess's amusement is tinged with anxiety. And indeed, the Count's arrival changes the atmosphere from laughter to fear.

Susanna has left. Cherubino, half undressed, hides in the dressing room. The Count demands to know who is in there. The Countess, terrified, says it is Susanna. The Count demands proof. Meanwhile Susanna slips back in, and unobserved, witnesses the drama. In this terzetto [21] Mozart again uses sonata form. But this time the tension is unrelieved. The music maintains its impetus, with the Count becoming increasingly enraged, and the two women more and more fearful. The sudden shifts from *p* to *f* serve to intensify the violence of the Count's emotions. When the Count storms out, taking his reluctant wife with him. Susanna and Cherubino have a quick whispered exchange before the page escapes by jumping from the window, and Susanna takes his place [22]. The Count, armed with tools to break down the door, returns with the Countess who, believing that all is lost, confesses that the person in the dressing room is Cherubino.

Now begins what is surely one of Mozart's most monumental achievements: the Finale to Act Two. In its scale, its complexity and its integration of dramatic and musical meaning, it is without precedent, and has never been surpassed. The range of the whole edifice may best be displayed in tabular form:

Scene Eight	Count and Countess/Duet	E flat major	*Allegro*	125 bars [24]
Scene Nine	Susanna enters/Terzet	B flat major	*Molto andante-allegro*	201 bars [25]
Scene Ten	Figaro enters/Quartet	G major	*Allegro*	69 bars [26]
		C major	*Andante*	68 bars [27]
Scene Eleven	Antonio enters/Quintet	F	*Allegro molto*	137 bars
		B flat major	*Andante*	[28]
Scene Twelve	Marcellina, Bartolo and Basilio enter/Septet	E flat major	*Allegro assai più allegro*	243 bars [29]

The musical structure has a rock-like solidity, an unbroken continuity and a totally symphonic breadth. It begins and ends with two massive sections in E flat major. In between it moves, as usual, first to the dominant key (B flat major), then it returns by a series of logical steps from G major to the home key. The sections are contrasted in tempo and metre, each one containing its own thematic material. All are related strictly to the evolution of the dramatic situation, as more detailed consideration will show.

The first scene is dominated by the Count. His rage increases as the Countess attempts to explain why he will find Cherubino in a state of undress. He denounces the Countess in biting accents and, despite her pleadings, is on the point of breaking down the door, when it opens, and out comes, not the page, but Susanna [25]. The musical change is magical. To the most innocent of minuet rhythms, played by strings alone, Susanna expresses her bewilderment at all the fuss. For different reasons, both Count and Countess are momentarily stunned. But they recover, and as they do the music quickens. The Count goes to check Susanna's story. Susanna reassures the Countess, who makes the most of the situation. The Count is appropriately contrite, and the section ends with all three in accord. The main thematic material consists of two contrasting themes heard in the orchestra which are fully developed during the scene.

At this crucial moment Figaro appears summoning the company to the wedding festivities in cheerful music [26] in a bright G major key. But the

Christian du Plessis as the Count and Eric Shilling as Antonio in the ENO production (photo: Anthony Crickmay)

Count sees the opportunity to get further confirmation of Susanna's story, and begins questioning his servant. Matching the insistent probing of the questioner and the hesitation of Figaro, the music changes key, and slows down [28]. With the prompting of the women Figaro fends off, but does not convince the Count, who looks for the arrival of Marcellina to enforce her legal rights on Figaro.

But the next arrival is Antonio, with his tale of a man jumping from the window onto his flower pots. This time it is Figaro's turn to improvise a story for the increasingly suspicious Count. Throughout the episode the orchestra keeps up a bubbling stream of triplets. Then the tempo assumes a more deliberate pace, as Antonio's tale becomes more circumstantial, and Figaro's ingenuity is stretched to the limit. He finally succeeds in giving satisfactory answers to all the Count's questions and his relief is matched by a triumphant resolution in the music [29]. But the final scene, in which Marcellina, Bartolo and Basilio erupt onto the stage, brings yet another change of fortune. Marcellina's legal rights are apparently inescapable, and all the manoeuvrings of Figaro and his allies are in vain. The Act is brought to a vivid musical climax involving all the principal characters in a septet.

The second act finale at Glyndebourne in 1938 with (left to right) Mariano Stabile, Aulikki Rautawaara, Audrey Mildmay, John Brownlee, Heddle Nash, Constance Willis and Salvatore Baccaloni (Theatre Museum)

Act Three opens with the continued weaving of the plot in recitative. In the duetto which follows, the Count presses the apparently complaisant Susanna, who is nervously distracted. To the Count's repeated questions she twice gives the wrong answer, and has to correct herself. The Count's insistence is well conveyed in the opening minor key, with its chromatic inflections [30], and his relief in the transition to the major [31]. Like so much else in the opera, the touching unanimity of the two characters in the closing bars has its ironical implications.

But the Count overhears a remark from Susanna to Figaro, and realises he is being duped. The accompaniment to his recitative lends weight and an ominous significance to his soliloquy. Although as a Count he has officially renounced his *droit de seigneur*, his arrogance as a man rebels at the idea that his servant may enjoy what he cannot, and the following aria expresses his feelings in violent terms. Mozart uses the stock-in-trade effects for such a situation: rushing unison scales, leaps, trills, dynamic contrasts, and a testing, wide-ranging vocal line [32, 33]. The aria reminds us of the underlying current of intolerance and violence, barely held in check, in the opera.

The sestetto that follows is another instance of entrancing situation comedy. Disguises, misunderstandings, unexpected revelations of identity are the very stuff of 18th-century opera. No example is more appropriately placed or wittily handled than this discovery that not only is Figaro the son of Marcellina; his father is none other than Bartolo. The scene begins with music of graceful tenderness [34], as Marcellina embraces her long-lost son, and Figaro responds. Strings and woodwind enhance the reunion with their counterpoints. Susanna's entry and incredulity leads to more agitated music [35]. But the peace of the opening returns as Marcellina explains the truth to her. Dramatically right, this return shows Mozart's consummate ability to vary the detail of his initial material on its return. The final passage shows Mozart's profound understanding of vocal ensemble and repays detailed consideration. According to Michael Kelly, who sang Don Curzio, the 'Stuttering Judge', in the first performance, this was Mozart's own favourite piece in the opera.

The next scene belongs to the Countess. Apprehensive about her role in the plot to expose the Count she recalls the days of their early untroubled love. Just as the Count's position and character were underlined by accompanied recitative, so here instrumental support is applied to extend the musings of the devoted but neglected Countess. And her second aria *'Dove sono'* ('I remember') [36] beautifully embodies the nobility and tenderness of her character. The simple melodic outline of the opening is embellished with gently leaning *appoggiaturas*, and supported by delicate touches of strings and wind. The mention of 'pain and sorrow' includes darker harmonies. But the opening mood returns and leads into a quick section in which she expresses her determination to win back her husband's affections.

Susanna rejoins the Countess, and they compose the note of assignation for the Count, Susanna writing to the Countess's dictation. Despite their difference in social rank, the two women are sisters under the skin, and this duet is utterly charming in its atmosphere of conspiratorial intimacy [37]. Against the quietly rocking string accompaniment the woodwind share the supple flowing melodic line with the two singers. Once again a duet gives us additional insight into two of the characters.

The mood of lightheartedness continues with the following chorus. The ingenuous singing of the village maidens is adorned by the orchestra, and the Countess gently mocks the disguised Cherubino. The advent of the Count changes the atmosphere again. His suspicions are again aroused; but Figaro, confident that the marriage will now take place, brushes them aside, and leads them into the wedding festivities that form the Finale of the Act.

Musically the Finale comprises three elements. The march [38] begins as a background to the continuing conversation. It is composed of the simplest thematic ideas, yet has its distinctive flavour distilled out of the harmony and the orchestration. Its effect is enhanced by the rise in dynamic level from a distant *pp* to a triumphant climax. The ensuing duet is carried along by its bustling accompaniment, and it too ends with a brilliant C major flourish.

In both of these pieces Mozart's imaginative economy of instrumentation is evident. But in this respect tha dance movement that follows surpasses them both [39]. The *fandango* is in origin a Spanish courtship dance. Like other dances of popular origin it rose in the world, and became fashionable among the aristocracy in the late 18th century. Gluck used a popular example in the ballet of *Don Juan* of 1781. Mozart took the same melody in a different guise, and incorporated it into this Finale. It is an extraordinarily haunting piece, stylised yet expressive, poised yet flowing. And never has a semitone been used more effectively that in the two note counterpoint reiterated by flute, oboe and

The third act finale in Jonathan Miller's ENO production designed by Patrick Robertson and Rosemary Vercoe (photo: Anthony Crickmay)

bassoon. Against this background Susanna gives the Count the letter she and the Countess have composed. As he opens it, he pricks his finger with the pin — a suggestive incident observed by Figaro. Then all join in the festivities, to the music of the duet and chorus.

The beginning of Act Four is in total contrast. Barbarina is searching for the lost pin, in a state of growing apprehension. The discrepancy between the apparently trivial loss and the emotion it induces has a comic dimension. But Barbarina's anxiety, conveyed precisely by the muted strings, the gently throbbing accompaniment, and the breathless, poignantly shaped phrases of the melodic line, is all too real.

The next aria is allocated to Marcellina. It is often omitted, which is doubly regrettable, as it is interesting in itself, and it allows Marcellina to be seen as a more positive figure. The choice of *Tempo di Menuetto* underlines her courtly aspirations, the sudden bursts of *coloratura* her slightly comic pretentiousness. And if she complains rather repetitiously about the perfidy of men, she may have her reasons. Basilio's aria, too, is rarely heard. He retells an amusing fable to explain his adoption of the pose of a fool. Rather long, this number is less to be regretted than its companion piece. Perhaps the smooth hypocrisy of the character is too innate, too subtle to be explained away in this manner.

Meanwhile the intrigue has developed. Figaro now suspects his wife of intended infidelity. He calls on Bartolo and Basilio to be discreet witnesses of her misconduct, and expresses his bitterness in a recitative and aria. This is his moment of strongest feeling, when he sees his situation, understandably from his point of view, as tragic. The string accompaniment in the recitative underlines his alternating grief and outrage.

In the aria he inveighs bitterly against the faithlessness of women, in strongly accented music of wide-ranging compass and angular leaps [41]. In the closing bars the horns add to his torment with their mocking comments. His state of mind is not improved when Susanna, realising he is within earshot, decides to confirm his suspicions. In her recitative and aria she expresses her impatience at her lover's delay, in music which combines simplicity and longing [42], with an accompaniment deftly scored for woodwind and pizzicato strings.

In the Finale all the complexities of the plot are unravelled. Cherubino declares his love to the Countess, thinking her to be Susanna [43]. He is discovered by the Count, and makes off. It is now the Count's turn to make advances to the supposed Susanna. But he too is interrupted, by Figaro. Figaro notices another woman, and is not deceived by Susanna's disguise. He turns the tables on her, by pretending to make love to her as the Countess. She attempts to maintain her impersonation, but her rising indignation gets the better of her, and she boxes the delighted Figaro's ear. He confesses that he recognised her, and together they determine to maintain the charade for the Count's benefit. The sight of his servant apparently making advances to his wife enrages him and he swears vengeance. But the real Countess abandons her disguise. The Count is shamed into begging his wife for forgiveness. This she grants, not for the first and probably not for the last time. The opera ends with general celebrations.

Each of Mozart's great operas has its unique personality; each helps us to understand some aspects of the human condition. *Don Giovanni* treats of love, lust and the destructive power of pride. *Così fan tutte* examines the connection between social mask and personal feeling. *The Magic Flute* explores the meaning of symbolism, the problem of putting idealism into practice. *The Marriage of Figaro* contains something of all of these; and more besides. It is a study of a wide range of individuals interacting in a recognisable social situation. That the range is so comprehensive, crossing social boundaries without obscuring them, is in the first instance due to the comprehensive perception of Beaumarchais, who created a sharply delineated group of personalities in complex, interlocking and developing relationships. The operatic collaborators, with an infallible certainty of touch, used their medium to humanise still further the writer's creations. The reduction of the intellectual dimension of the play is more than compensated for by the extraordinarily real emotional interplay in the opera. It is the combination of variety, vividness and naturalness of characterisation that makes *Figaro*, for many, the most memorable, most exhilarating, and the greatest of all social comedies.

Pauline Lucca who first sang Cherubino at Covent Garden in 1866 (Theatre Museum)

Ava June as the Countess in the 1965 Sadler's Wells production by John Blatchley, designed by Vivienne Kernot and conducted by Charles Mackerras (photo: Reg Wilson)

Music and Comedy in 'The Marriage of Figaro'

Stephen Oliver

Explaining the point of other people's jokes is a dreary business: but do not be alarmed, I do not mean to do quite that. After all, Mozart's individual strokes of humour are models of clarity. We all rejoice in the Count's discovery of Cherubino hiding in the armchair; and it is not until we have stopped laughing that we realize with what meticulous care the moment has been exposed for us. No sudden shock; no whisking off the covers; no great bangs on the orchestra: but slow, soft, creeping music, as the people on the stage gradually realize the significant ironies of the situation. This realisation needs time; and Mozart gives it plenty of time. He even allows us to laugh without having to drown a single word, by putting a silent pause after Basilio's incomparable:

And this sense of clarity pays dividends when Mozart is dealing with purely verbal jokes. In a comedy about marriage and sex, it's not surprising that now and then his characters make suggestive remarks, like the Count's

or Figaro's

To make sure everyone picks up the words at these points, nothing in the least elaborate is permitted to get in the way of the text. The orchestra merely plays along with the voice part in octaves. But these plain octaves themselves take on significance. They somehow sound salacious; it's perhaps something to do with the very careful off-beat phrasing of:

Here, what doubtless began as a technical device — a method of getting the words over clearly — ends as a dramatic reinforcement. The octaves admirably express the over-significant tone — 'Nudge, nudge, wink, wink' — that people adopt at such moments.

Marie McLaughlin as Susanna and Patricia Payne as Marcellina at Covent Garden in the 1980/81 season (photo: Donald Southern)

We recognize the tone of voice here — we have all made such jokes in just such a way. And this recognition makes the music real to us as well as funny. It is like that moment when Susanna harps on Marcellina's age:

Your age! your age! your age!

We recognize the rhetoric of the playground:

Cowar - dy cowar - dy cus - tard!

and are amused, and perhaps a little ashamed of ourselves as well.

This makes for great comedy, this touching as well as amusing us — and we can all pick out moments in *Figaro* where we are touched and delighted at the same time like that. My own favourite, for what it's worth, is the self-disgust and embarrassment of Figaro's interruption of his own cadence in his Act Four aria:

What happens you all of you know: —— the rest we'll pass ov-er in si - lence.

That stabbing high Db (x marks the spot in my example) as another wave of shame and anger breaks over him is horribly real.

But these are all individual moments; and merely stringing such insights together will not make an opera. So what is it that makes *Figaro* — the whole opera — so satisfactory, so amusing, so invigorating a work?

We think at first of tunes. How could an opera with such tunes as *'Dove sono', 'Voi che sapete',* and *'Deh vieni'* in it be anything other than a masterpiece? Well, it may be heresy to say so, but I don't think Mozart's melodies, simply as melodies, to be uniquely beautiful. They are distinguished, of course; incomparably orchestrated and finished: but the achievement of the tunes themselves can be equalled in many another eighteenth-century opera.

If it is not the tunes or the individual jokes alone that make the music of this opera so satisfying, what is it then? We open the score: the conductor raises his baton: and the *pianissimo* quavers begin (See page 00 [1]). Consider for a moment that phrase which opens the Overture. Apart from anything else, merely as the start of an overture it's unusual enough. Most comic operas before or since have begun their overtures with a loud bang, not with this soft surreptitious scurrying of mere surprise. It is rapid, secretive; the music of intrigues and whispers. There is a suggestion of harmonic tension too — when the phrase is repeated twenty seconds later, the woodwind provide a discord on every main beat. And this tension immediately explodes in a loud answering phrase, itself sufficiently discordant:

The way the music proceeds, in fact, is by building up tensions and immediately releasing them, those releases themselves becoming a source for new tensions. The music is, literally, progressive — not in the sense that it is modern for its time; but in that it is built so that it never relaxes, because each phrase is always pressing forward into the next.

But doesn't all music work like that? Am I merely imagining this particular source of tension? Look at another Mozart overture, superficially built on the same lines — that to *Così fan tutte*. It begins quite differently; here, indeed, we have the conventional loud opening in the easiest of harmonic styles, merely alternating between tonic and dominant. But even when it starts sounding a bit like *Figaro* — in the following fast section — the likeness is only superficial. The actual musical phrases, to be sure, are not at all unlike those of *Figaro* — a soft rapid movement round a note followed by loud passages with trumpets and drums. But the tension of the *Figaro* harmony is not in the *Così* overture at all — in *Così*, the strings frankly settle down to an easy um-cha-cha-cha rhythm, and the woodwind merely chuckle above them.

Or for an even clearer example of the way tension is built into the music of *Figaro*, compare its opening scene with that of *Così*. *Così* actually begins with a quarrel; and here, at any rate, you might expect the music to be tense and energetic. Not at all: the opening tune blandly outlines the common chord:

Irmgard Seefried as Susanna at Covent Garden in 1949 (photo: Richardby)

Turn in contrast to *Figaro*. The curtain goes up. A domestic scene: a man measuring a room, a girl trying on a hat. Nothing like a quarrel or even an argument. But listen to the music. Every phrase has a discord built into it — this sort of thing:

and later this:

And by such means a sense of tension is continually kept up throughout the whole duet.

You will have seen for some time what I'm driving at. I believe *Figaro* to be so satisfying an experience not just because of the tunes or the jokes, agreeable

Agnes Baltsa as Cherubino and Hermann Prey as Figaro at Covent Garden in 1977. (photo: Christina Burton)

as they are. Rather it is because the texture of the music is so highly wrought — works at so high a level of tension — that the energy thus generated presses us through the opera's considerable length with an unremitting sense of expectation and delight. The opera remains exciting because of the tensions generated by the music.

Why, after all, did the audience at the first dress rehearsal of Act One, in 1786, go so wild at the end of *'Non più andrai'* ('Say goodbye now to pastime and play'), its final number? Of course, it's something of an applause-catcher in itself, with its trumpets and drums and shouts of *'Cherubino alla vittoria!'* But in its context it carries a more formidable effect.

Every number in the first act has been pitched at a high level of excitement. To start with, over half of them are dramatic ensembles of one sort or another, in which the action sweeps forward. But even the solo songs are highly energised. The elegant measured rhythm of the minuet becomes explosive in Figaro's 'If you are after a little amusement'. Horns and plucked strings combine to paint a remarkable picture of suppressed resentment. The off-beat clarinets and chromatically rising strings of 'Is it pain, is it pleasure?' vividly convey Cherubino's constant state of sensual arousal. And the trumpets and drums of Bartolo's old-fashioned peroration build up the tension of the moment when joined with the furious pace of his patter. Even the little chorus, quaintly pastoral though it is, becomes a dangerous weapon in the struggle between Figaro and his master.

At the end of all this screwing up of tension comes 'Say goodbye now to pastime and play'. Here, the tune is simplicity itself, merely outlining the chords on which it's based. The phrase lengths are evenly balanced, and mostly grouped in pairs. There is no chromaticism; and the modulations are of the most obvious kind. The rondo form is simple and clear. Everything in the song is straightforward and direct. And thus, with a rush, the tension of the whole Act is released. The simple idea of a vigorous, martial tune, combined with its placing at the end of a complicated Act, makes its effect doubly strong. Music and drama fuse together in a moment of theatrical power possible only to opera.

No wonder the audience at that dress rehearsal, obscurely recognizing this, leapt up with cries of congratulation; and the little man, smiling ecstatically, bowed again and again from his seat at the harpsichord. To have brought off so complicated and subtle an effect and to do it with such apparent simplicity and ease is a mark of the highest skill. Doubtless Mozart, if not his audience, knew that perfectly well.

And I must not forget that this skill is here addressing itself to the purposes of comedy. For *Figaro* is extremely funny; and funny because of the intensity and energy of the music. Whether it is the accompanying triplets of 'I bid you good-day, ma'am' surging to the top of the texture as the two women exchange insults; or the deliberate, constant, almost menacing tread of the fandango bass as letters are passed and fingers are pricked; or the horns — cuckold's horns — jeering at poor Figaro as he inveighs against all women — it is always the power of the music that makes the comedy. It has often been pointed out, for instance, how the romantic beauty of Susanna's *'Deh, vieni'* ('Then come, my heart's delight') creates, by its being overheard by Figaro, a highly charged irony. For although Figaro thinks otherwise, it is really he whom Susanna is serenading, after all.

This brings us, indeed, to the other main way by which the music provides for the comedy. *Figaro* is at some moments a farcical play, rapidly moving from situation to situation; so energy and tension in the music is very much to be desired. But it is also a play about love, about feeling; and this, not in the mere writing of tunes, is really where the richness and elegance of Mozart's language finds its purpose. The Countess's song *'Porgi amor'* ('God of Love') begins, oddly, with the same phrase as the bustling *'Se a caso, madama'* ('Supposing one evening') of the first act. But the discord which gave the earlier tune impetus:

Sup - pos - ing one eve - ning mi - (lady)

now becomes a faintly self-indulgent sigh, wonderfully extended in its answering phrase:

God of love, — I now im - plore you...

The energy generated by the discord is still there, but transmuted to romantic sentiment.

By the Letter Duet in Act Three, though, all harmonic tension has disappeared. The music is as sweet as Mozart can make it; and the comedy lies wholly in the irony of the situation. The two women seek to trick the husband of one of them into decent behaviour by tempting him to adultery with the other. 'He'll understand that well enough', they say; and the setting of the remark by Mozart changes its bitterness into an inevitable and accepted sorrow.

34

The music, in other places informing the situation with energy, here provides a moment of reflective beauty. It is by these two ways that the comedy as comedy finally lives. The jokes, the tunes, the natural turns of speech are all subsumed in music of equal energy and loveliness.

And this is surely an odd thing. Everyone knows that Beaumarchais's *Figaro* was a conventional type of plot brought to new life, partly by injecting a little romantic sensibility into it, to be sure, but mostly by injecting a great deal of savage social satire. This whole comic method — the oldest indeed of comic methods, extending certainly back to Aristophanes — Mozart calmly ignores. There is practically no social satire in the opera. Mozart was far too absorbed in the contemplation of his people, his Count and Countess, his gardeners and chambermaids and pages, to satirise them. No doubt he had his own views on their behaviour, but they cannot be said to intrude upon the opera. Merely presenting his people as vividly as he can will be interesting and amusing enough.

Here falls into place one of Mozart's purely arbitrary pieces of luck. He was working at a time when people still enjoyed the old comedies of situation, requiring them merely to be infused with good feeling to be made new. Nothing could have been more fortunate for an opera composer. He had no need to waste time setting up conventions; the conventions were well understood: and he could confine himself to filling them with what new life his genius prompted him to. Too much life for his contemporaries, perhaps — 'Too many notes, my dear Mozart' said Emperor Leopold — but for us the energy and temper of the music make of the comedy's rather faded colours an invigorating and enduring delight.

Kiri te Kanawa (as the Countess) and Reri Grist (as Susanna) in John Copley's production at Covent Garden (photo: Reg Wilson)

Tito Gobbi as the Count and Joan Carlyle as the Countess at Covent Garden in 1967 (photo: Donald Southern)

Sumner Austin as the Count and Joan Cross as the Countess in the famous 1934 Sadler's Wells production by Clive Carey designed by Rex Whistler (Joan Cross Collection)

Beaumarchais's Characters

These descriptions appeared in many editions of the play.

Figaro ... If the actor sees in this role anything other than good sense seasoned with gaiety and sallies of wit — above all, if he introduces any element of caricature — he will diminish the effect of a role which, in the opinion of Monsieur Préville, the leading comic actor of our theatre, would bring honour to the talents of any player able to appreciate the fine shades of the part and fully rise to the opportunities it offers.

Suzanne. She is a resourceful, intelligent, and lively young woman, but she has none of the almost brazen gaiety characteristic of some of our young actresses who play maidservants.

Marceline. She is a woman of intelligence and of naturally lively temperament but the errors of her youth and subsequent experience have chastened her.

Chérubin. This part can only be played, as it was in fact, by a young and very pretty woman: we have no very young men in our theatre who are at the same time sufficiently mature to appreciate the fine points of the part. Chérubin is diffident in the extreme in the presence of the Countess but otherwise he is a charming young scamp. The basis of his character is an undefined and restless desire. He is entering on adolescence all unheeding and with no understanding of what is happening to him, and throws himself eagerly into everything that comes along. In fact, he is what every mother, in her innermost heart, would wish her own son to be even though he might give her much cause for suffering.

Count Almaviva should be played with great dignity yet with grace and affability. The depravity of his morals should in no way detract from the elegance of his manners. It was customary in those days for great noblemen to treat any design upon the fair sex in a spirit of levity. The part is all the more difficult to play well in that it is always the unsympathetic role.

The Countess. Torn between two conflicting emotions she should display only a restrained tenderness and very moderate degree of resentment, above all nothing which might impair her amiable and virtuous character in the eyes of the audience.

from the translation of the play by John Wood

Eilene Hannan as Susanna and Neil Howlett as the Count in the 1982 ENO production (photo John Haynes)

Teresa Stratas as Susanna in disguise, at Covent Garden (photo: Christina Burton)

Thematic Guide

Many of the themes from the opera have been identified in the articles by numbers in square brackets, which refer to the themes set out on these pages. The themes are also identified by the numbers in brackets at the corresponding points in the libretto, so that the words can be related to the musical themes.

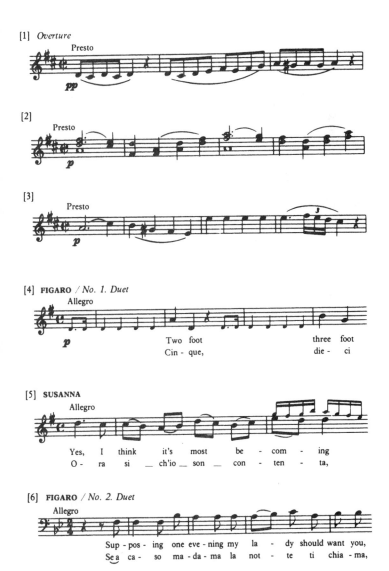

[1] *Overture*
Presto
pp

[2]
Presto
p

[3]
Presto
p

[4] **FIGARO** / *No. 1. Duet*
Allegro
p
Two foot   three foot
Cin - que,   die - ci

[5] **SUSANNA**
Allegro
Yes, I think it's most be - com - ing
O - ra si __ ch'io __ son __ con - ten - ta,

[6] **FIGARO** / *No. 2. Duet*
Allegro
Sup - pos - ing one eve - ning my la - dy should want you,
Se a ca - so ma - da - ma la not - te ti chia - ma,

39

[7] **FIGARO** / *No. 3. Cavatina*

Allegretto

If you are af - ter a lit - tle a - muse - ment
Se vuol bal - la - re, si - gnor Con - ti - no,

[8] **FIGARO**

Presto

Try to de - ceive me, I'll do the same thing
L'ar - te scher - men - do, l'ar - te a - do - pran - do,

[9] **BARTOLO** *No. 4. Aria*

Allegro con spirito

Now for ven - geance! ah, now for ven - geance!
La ven - det - ta, oh, la ven - det - ta!

[10] **BARTOLO**

Allegro con spirito

Once I can seize on the right op - por - tu - ni - ty,
Se tut - to il co - di - ce do - ves - si vol - ge - re,

[11] **CHERUBINO** *No. 6. Aria*

Allegro vivace

Is it pain, is it plea - sure that fills me,
Non so piu co - sa son, co - sa fac - cio,

[12] **COUNT** *No. 7. Trio*

Allegro assai

How dis - grace - ful! Go at once Sir,
Co - sa sen - to! To - sto an - da - te,

[13] *No. 7. Trio*

[a] **BASILIO**   [b] **SUSANNA**

Allegro assai

My in - tru - sion brought con - fu - sion; Oh, how dreadful I am ru - in'd

[14] **PEASANTS** / *No. 8a. Chorus*

Allegro

Come, lads and lass - es flow - ers hum - bly strew - ing
Gio - va - ni lie - te, fio - ri spar - ge - te

FIGARO / *No. 9. Aria*

Vivace

Say good - bye now to pas - time and play, lad,
Non piu an - drai, far - fal - lo - ne a - mo - ro - so,

[16] **FIGARO**

Vivace

Yes, you'll find it quite ex - cit - ing,
Per mon - ta - gne, per val - lo - ni,

[17] **COUNTESS** / *No. 10. Cavatina*

Larghetto

God of love, I now im - plore thee,
Por - gi, a - mor, _____ qual - che ri - sto - ro,

[18] **CHERUBINO** / *No. 11. Canzona*

Andante con moto

Tell me, fair la - dies, tell me, oh tell
Voi, che sa - pe - te che co - sa e a - mor,

[19] **SUSANNA** / *No. 12. Aria*

Allegretto

Come here, and kneel im - med - iate - ly,
Ve - ni - te, in - gi - noc - chia - te - vi,

[20]

Allegretto

If wo - men all go mad for him, They have good rea - son why,
Se l'a - ma - no le fe - mi - ne, han cer - to il lor per - che!

[21] **COUNT** / *No. 13. Trio*

Allegro spirituoso

Come out, come out, Su - san - na,
Su - san - na, or via sor - ti - te!

[22] **SUSANNA** / *No. 14. Duet*

Allegro assai

Be quick, un - lock the door now, it's on - ly me, Su - san - na,
A - pri - te, pre - sto a - pri - te, a - pri - te, e la Su - san - na,

COUNT / *No. 15 Finale*

Allegro

Out you come, no more con - ceal - ment
E - scio - mai, gar - zon mal - na - to;

[24]

COUNTESS Ah, how blind his jeal - ous pas __ sion!
Ah! la cie - ca __ ge - lo - si - a,

Allegro

COUNT I'll have ven-geance,
Mo - ra, mo- ra!

[25] **SUSANNA**

Your ser - vant!
Si - gno - re!

Molto andante

[26] **FIGARO**

Allegro

My lord and my la - dy, the mu - sic is rea - dy,
Si - gno - re, di fuo - ri son gia i suo - na - to - ri,

[27] **COUNT**

Andante

Here's a let - ter, mas- ter Fi - ga - ro, have you seen it once be - fore?
Co - no - sce - te, si - gnor Fi - ga - ro, que - sto fo - glio chi ver - go?

[28]

Andante

[29] **MARCELLINA, BASILIO, BARTOLO**

Allegro assai

We ap - pear be - fore your lord-ship,
Voi, si - gnor, che giu - sto sie - te,

[30] **COUNT** *No. 16. Duet*

Andante

Oh, why are you so cru - el, why _____ must I ask in vain?
Cru - del! per - che fi - no - ra far- mi lan - guir co - si?

42

[31]

Andante

Oh joy, past _____ all ex - press - ing
Mi sen - to _____ dal con - ten - to

[32] **COUNT** / No. 17. Aria

Allegro maestoso

Must I for - go my plea - sure, while serf of mine re - joic - es?
Ve - dro men-tr'io so - spi - ro, fe - li - ce un ser - vo mi - o!

[33] **COUNT**

Allegro assai

I will en - dure no long - er Ven - geance a - lone in - spires me,
Gia la spe - ran - za so - la del - le ven - det - te mi - e

[34] **MARCELLINA** / No. 18. Sextet

Andante

Oh, my long - lost child, em - brace me, let your mo - ther's arms en - fold you!
Ri - co - no - sci in que - sto am - ples - so u - na ma - dre, a - ma - to fi - glio!

[35]

BARTOLO His mo - ther!
Sua ma - dre!

COUNT His mo - ther!
Sua ma - dre!

Andante

SUSANNA His mo - ther?
Sua ma - dre?

SUSANNA His mo - ther?
Sua ma - dre?

CURZIO His mo - ther!
Sua ma - dre!

MARCELLINA His mo - ther!
Sua ma - dre!

SUSANNA His mo - ther?
Sua ma - dre?

SUSANNA His mo - ther!
Sua ma - dre!

[36] **COUNTESS** / No. 19. Aria

Andantino

I re - mem - ber days long de - part - ed,
Do - ve so - no i bei mo - men - ti,

[37] **COUNTESS** / from No. 20. Duet

Allegretto

How de - light - ful 'tis to wan - der
Che so - a - ve ze - fi - ret - to,

[38] *Wedding March*

Marcia

pp

[39] *Fandango*

Andante *tr*

p

[40] **BARBARINA** / *No. 23. Cavatina*

Andante

I have lost it. Oh how dread - ful, Oh, where e - ver can it be?
L'ho per - du - ta, me me - schi - na! ah chi sa do - ve sa - ra,

[41] **FIGARO** / *No. 26. Aria*

Moderato

Yes, fools you are, and will be,   fools, till your eyes are o - pen'd
A - pri - te un po' quegl' oc - chi,   Uo - mi - ni in - cau - ti e scioc - chi.

[42] **SUSANNA** / *No. 27. Aria*

Andante

p Then come,   my heart's de - light,   no more - de - lay - ing
Deh, vie - ni, non tar - dar,   o gio - ja bel - la.

[43] **CHERUBINO**

Andante

p   *sfp*

Soft - ly soft - ly I'll ap - proach her
Pian, pia - nin le an - dro piu pres - so,

[44] **FIGARO**

Andante

p Now Su - san - na, be kind and for - give me;
Pa - ce, pa - ce, mio dol - ce te - so - ro!

The Marriage of Figaro
Le Nozze di Figaro

Opera Comica in Four Acts by Wolfgang Amadeus Mozart
Text by Lorenzo da Ponte after Beaumarchais's
La Folle Journée ou Le Mariage de Figaro
English version by Edward J. Dent

Le Nozze di Figaro was first performed in Vienna on May 1, 1786. The first performance in England was at the King's Theatre, Haymarket on June 18, 1812 (and in English at Covent Garden on March 6, 1819). The first performance in the United States was in New York on May 10, 1824.

The autograph score of the first two acts is now in East Berlin; the last two acts are (since World War II) in the Biblioteka Jagiellońska in Kraków. It shows the revisions made for the 1789 revival to accommodate da Ponte's mistress Adriana del Bene as Susanna: her heroic voice must have been quite different from that of Nancy Storace, the soprano who had created the role three years before. Mozart set two new passages: *'Un moto di gioia'* to replace *'Venite inginocchiatevi'*, and the impressive rondò *'Al desio di chi t'adora'* for *'Deh, vieni, non tardar'*. The autograph also shows that although the Countess originally had the upper line and Susanna the lower throughout all ensembles, Mozart altered this, irrespective of dramatic sense, later (possibly for this 1789 revival). Sir Charles Mackerras has, since the 1965 Sadler's Wells production, reverted to the original intention, maintaining that, particularly in certain passages of Act Two, it is important for the Countess to dominate the ensemble, while Susanna and Figaro sing together (bars 824-833; 880-891).

In preparing this libretto of *Le Nozze di Figaro*, we began with the edition made by Paolo Lecaldano for Rizzoli (*Tre Libretti per Mozart*, Milan, 1956). There, da Ponte's autograph version is presented with carefully systematised stage-directions, modernised and consistent spellings, and regular punctuation. His aim was to produce an accurate version of the literary text. We have varied from this where the text differs from what Mozart finally set to music. While the layout and stage-directions follow the original libretto as far as possible, we have reverted to certain archaisms of spelling and inserted Mozart's words in order to present what is actually sung. The stage directions have very occasionally been supplemented by those in the score, where there is no indication at all in the libretto. As such, they represent no actual production and do not form part of Dent's translation.

The translation, made for Lilian Baylis's company at the Old Vic, and first performed there (with spoken dialogue) on January 15, 1920, has naturally been extensively revised over the years, and these current revisions are incorporated.

The numbers in square brackets refer to the Thematic Guide, and the numbers in italics are the numbers in the score. The braces in the margin show where characters sing together.

Preface

The time prescribed by Custom for dramatic performances, a certain established number of characters which may generally be practicable, and certain other sensible attitudes and conventions regarding the manners, the place and the audience, were the reasons why I did not make a translation of this excellent comedy, but rather a copy, or, one should say, an extract.

For this I was constrained to reduce the sixteen characters of the original to eleven, two of which can be played by the same person, and to omit, apart from one whole act, many delightful scenes, and many witty turns of phrase which are scattered through it: in their place I have substituted canzonettas, arias, choruses and other thoughts and words suitable for music: things that poetry alone, and never prose, can supply.

In spite, however, of all the zeal and care on the part of both the composer and myself to be brief, the opera will not be one of the shortest that has been performed on our stages. We hope that our excuse will be the variety of development of this drama, the length and scope of the same, the number of musical pieces necessary in order not to keep the performers idle, to avoid the boredom and monotony of the long recitatives, to paint faithfully and in full colour the diverse passions that are aroused, and to realize our special purpose, which was to offer a new type of spectacle, as it were, to a public of such refined taste and such assured understanding. — The Poet

A Note on Act Three

This sequence of scenes in Act Three follows the libretto and score. Robert Moberly and Christopher Raeburn suggested in 1965, however, that this does not represent the original intentions of da Ponte and Mozart. Their reasons, spelt out in an article in *Music and Letters* (April, 1965), convinced Sir Charles Mackerras enough to adopt the new sequence at Sadler's Wells, and this has been followed ever since by ENO at the London Coliseum, as well as by other conductors at the Royal Opera House, other theatres and on modern recordings.

	Traditional Order	Moberly / Raeburn Order
Scene Four	Hai già vinta la causa?	Hai già vinta la causa?
Scene Five	È decisa la lite:	Andiamo, andiam, bel paggio:
Scene Six	Eccovi, o caro amico,	E Susanna non vien!
Scene Seven	Andiamo, andiam, bel paggio:	È decisa la lite:
Scene Eight	E Susanna non vien!	Eccovi, o caro amico
Scene Nine	Io vi dico, signor	Io vi dico, signor

Because at the first performance Francesco Bussani sang the roles of both Bartolo and Antonio, some time had to be allowed for him to change clothes between *'Eccovi, o caro amico'* and *'Io vi dico, signor'*. There are indications in the text that these scenes followed one another, and that the little scene for Barbarina and Cherubino, and the Countess's scene, were rearranged at a late stage in the plan. This traditional rearrangement causes the frequent criticism that this act is less well constructed than the previous ones. The indications are as follows:

a) The Count would by convention be expected to leave the stage after a formal aria (*'Hai già vinta la causa?'*) as the Countess later does after hers.

b) It is also curious that Cherubino and Barbarina have no sooner left the stage than Cherubino's clothes are spotted by Antonio at the cottage.

c) There is little time for a trial off-stage between Figaro's exit in Scene Three and *'È decisa la lite'*.

d) It is odd that Susanna and the Countess do not apparently meet until after *'E Susanna non vien!'* Susanna, who would naturally have looked for her after seeing the Count in Scene Three, runs in with the Countess's dowry in the trial scene and leaves that scene with the others on purpose to look for her.

As Moberly and Raeburn write: 'If a piece of a jig-saw fits well in one place and badly in another place, one does not assume that the jig-saw designer meant it to fit badly.' Their solution has the advantage of despatching Barbarina and Cherubino earlier, and also introducing the Countess earlier. Her natural anxiety to know the outcome of Susanna's interview with the Count (*'E Susanna non vien!'*) is more appropriate (and less confusing for an audience) immediately she thinks it must have finished, rather than after the complications of the trial. Her 'exit aria' is thus juxtaposed with the Count's and precedes the comic complexities of the later part of the act.

In an article on the opera in *The Musical Times* (July, 1981) Alan Tyson discusses this sequence of scenes in the light of the evidence of the autograph score.

47

THE CHARACTERS

Count Almaviva *a Spanish nobleman* (Grande di Spagna)	*baritone*
Countess Almaviva *his wife*	*soprano*
Susanna *the Countess's maid, promised in marriage to*	*soprano*
Figaro *the Count's man-servant*	*bass*
Cherubino *the Count's page*	*soprano*
Marcellina *a governess*	*soprano*
Bartolo *a Doctor of Seville*	*bass*
Basilio *a music teacher*	*tenor*
Don Curzio *a judge*	*tenor*
Barbarina *daughter of*	*soprano*
Antonio *the Count's gardener and Susanna's uncle*	*bass*
Chorus of Countrymen and Women	
Chorus of Various Other Classes of People	

The action takes place in the house of Count Almaviva (which Beaumarchais had named Aguas Frescas and located three leagues from Seville).

Graziella Sciutti as Susanna and Pilar Lorengar as the Countess in the 1958 Glyndebourne production by Carl Ebert, designed by Oliver Messel (photo: Guy Gravett)

Act One

An unfurnished room* with a large arm-chair in the centre.

<u>Scene One.</u> *Susanna and Figaro. / No. 1. Duet*

FIGARO
(measuring the room)

Two foot, three foot, four foot, five foot, [4]	Cinque . . . dieci . . . venti . . . trenta .
That makes six foot, just six foot three.	Trentasei . . . quarantatré . . .

SUSANNA
(aside, looking at herself in a mirror trying on a hat decorated with flowers)

Yes, I think it's most becoming, [5]	Ora sì ch'io son contenta:
Just the sort of hat for me.	Sembra fatto inver per me.

(to Figaro, still admiring herself)

Do look here, my darling Figaro,	Guarda un po', mio caro Figaro,
Don't you think my hat is lovely?	Guarda <u>adesso</u> il mio cappello.

FIGARO

Yes, I'm sure it suits you nicely,	Sì, mio core, or è più bello:
Just the hat I like to see.	Sembra <u>fatto inver</u> per te.

SUSANNA AND FIGARO

There's a hat for a bride at a wedding,	Ah, il mattino alle nozze vicino
There's a hat for a bride to be proud of,	Quant' è dolce al' { mio / tuo } tenero sposo
There's a hat! And { my / your } little Susanna	Questo bel <u>cappellino</u> vezzoso
Made it all by herself as you see.	Che Susanna ella <u>stessa</u> si fe'.

Recitative

SUSANNA

Tell me, what are you measuring	Cosa stai <u>misurando</u>,
There, Figaro darling?	Caro il mio Figaretto?

FIGARO

I'm thinking about the bed which	Io guardo se quel letto,
His <u>lordship</u> said he'd give us,	Che ci destina il Conte,
To see which is the best place to put it.	Farà buona figura in questo <u>loco</u>.

SUSANNA

But, not in this room?	In questa stanza?

FIGARO

Surely: this is the room	Certo: a noi la cede
My lord himself has donated.	Generoso il padrone.

SUSANNA

You may sleep here alone then.	Io per me te la dono.

FIGARO

What's your objection?	E la <u>ragione</u>?

SUSANNA
(tapping her forehead)

I have reason enough.	La ragione l'ho qui.

FIGARO
(doing the same)

Then why won't you say	Perchè non puoi
What your reason may be?	Far che <u>passi</u> un po' qui.

---

* The score has 'a half-unfurnished room'.

Why should I tell you?	Perchè non voglio.
Aren't you my humble servant?	Sei tu mio servo, o no?

FIGARO

Yours to command, ma'am;	Ma non capisco
But I can see a reason	Perchè tanto ti spiace
For refusing a room that's so convenient.	La più commoda stanza del palazzo.

SUSANNA

Because I am Susanna, and you are a blockhead.	Perch'io son la Susanna, e tu sei pazzo.

FIGARO

Thank you, you're far too flattering.	Grazie: non tanti elogi. Guarda un poco,
But now tell me, could you find any room to suit us better?	Se potria meglio stare in altro loco.

No. 2. Duet

Supposing one evening	[6]	Se a caso Madama
My lady should want you.		La notte ti chiama:
Ting, ting! What a long way		Din, din, in due passi
You found it before!		Da quella puoi gir.

Or else if I'm rung for	Vien poi l'occasione
To go to his lordship:	Che vuolmi il padrone:
Dong, dong! in three steps	Don, don, in tre salti
I am there at his door!	Lo vado a servir.

SUSANNA

Supposing his lordship	Così se il mattino
One morning should send you,	Il caro Contino:
Ting, ting! on a message	Din, din, e ti manda
Some five miles away;	Tre miglia lontan;
Dong, dong! There's a way too	Don, don, a mia porta
That he will find shorter,	Il diavol lo porta,
He's here in a moment ...	Ed ecco in tre salti ...

FIGARO

Susanna, no more.	Susanna, pian, pian.

SUSANNA

Now listen.	Ascolta.

FIGARO

Quick, tell me!	Fa' presto.

SUSANNA

I'll tell you a secret,	Se udir brami il resto,
But don't be suspicious	Discaccia i sospetti
Or jealous again.	Che torto mi fan.

FIGARO

I must hear your secret,	Udir bramo il resto:
The cause of suspicion	I dubbi, i sospetti
Is only too plain.	Gelare mi fan.

Recitative

SUSANNA

Be quiet, and then I'll tell you.	Orbene, ascolta e taci.

FIGARO
(*disturbed*)

Well then, what is your secret?	Parla, che c'è di nuovo?

SUSANNA

His noble lordship,	Il signor Conte,
Finds he is tired of hunting all the country	Stanco di andar cacciando le straniere

For amorous adventures;
So he means to come home now,
In the hope of a new one.
But it is not the Countess, let me tell you,
That his lordship is after.

Bellezze forastiere,
Vuole ancor nel castello
Ritentar la sua sorte;
Nè già di sua consorte, bada bene,
Appetito gli viene.

FIGARO

Who is it this time?   E di chi, dunque?

SUSANNA

Why, your dear little Susanna.   Della tua Susannetta.

FIGARO
(surprised)

What, you?   Di te?

SUSANNA

The very same, sir, and you can see now
How useful he will find it
If he gives us a room where I'm his
neighbour.

Di me medesma. Ed ha speranza
Che al nobil suo progetto
Utilissima sia tal vicinanza.

FIGARO

Bravo! And what's the next thing?   Bravo! Tiriamo avanti.

SUSANNA

Now you can understand the real meaning
Of the gracious protection that he shows us.

Queste le grazie son, questa la cura
Ch'egli prende di te, della tua sposa.

FIGARO

I do indeed. How very altruistic!   Oh, guarda un po' che carità pelosa!

SUSANNA

That's not all; there's more to tell you. Don
Basilio,
Who teaches me singing, is in the plot too,
And loses no occasion
To inform me of this at every lesson.

Chetati: or viene il meglio. Don Basilio,
Mio maestro di canto e suo *factotum*,
Nel darmi la lezione
Mi ripete ogni dì questa canzone.

FIGARO

What, Basilio? Oh, the scoundrel!   Chi? Basilio? Oh, birbante!

SUSANNA

Did you suppose then   E tu credevi
My lord gave me a dowry
Just to reward your service?

Che fosse la mia dote
Merto del tuo bel muso?

FIGARO

I had flattered myself so.   Me n'era lusingato.

SUSANNA

Oh no, he gave it   Ei la destina
To buy from me that old established
privilege
Which the Lord of the Manor . . .

Per ottener da me certe mezz'ore
Che il diritto feudale . . .

FIGARO

Privilege! Has not my lord himself
Abolished it for ever?

Come! ne' feudi suoi
Non l'ha il Conte abolito?

SUSANNA

He has, but regrets it; and he would like to
Buy it back again from me.

Ebben, ora è pentito; e par che tenti
Riscattarlo da me.

FIGARO

Would he? I like that!   Bravo! mi piace!
That's what I call a nobleman:
He just does what he likes. I think he'll find
that . . .

Che caro signor Conte!
Ci vogliam divertir: trovato avete . . .

(A bell rings.)

Who's ringing? It's the Countess.	Chi suona? La Contessa.

SUSANNA

Then I must leave you. Good-bye, Figaro darling.	Addio, addio, addio, Figaro bello.

FIGARO

We'll hold our own against them.	Coraggio, mio tesoro.

SUSANNA

Keep your wits about you.	E tu, cervello.

(Exit.)

Scene Two. *Figaro alone.*

FIGARO
(pacing angrily up and down the room and rubbing his hands together)

I thank your lordship kindly! Now I'm beginning	Bravo, signor padrone! Ora incomincio
To understand all this mystery and to appreciate	A capir il mistero . . . e a veder schietto
Your most generous intentions. And so to London;	Tutto il vostro progetto: a Londra, è vero?
You ambassador, I as courier, and my Susanna,	Voi ministro, io corriero, e la Susanna
'Confidential attachée'!	Segreta ambasciatrice . . .
No, I'm hanged if she does. Figaro knows better!	Non sarà, non sarà: Figaro il dice.

No. 3. Cavatina

If you are after A little amusement, You may go dancing, I'll play the tune.	[7]	Se vuol ballare, Signor Contino, Il chitarrino Le suonerò.
I'll teach your lordship Steps and deportment, New kinds of capers You shall learn soon.		Se vuol venire Nella mia scuola, La capriola Le insegnerò.
You shall never doubt it, But in my own way I'll set about it; I've got my plan.		Saprò . . . Ma, piano: Meglio ogni arcano, Dissimulando, Scoprir potrò.
Try to deceive me, I'll do the same thing; Two play at that game, Yes, Sir, believe me, I'll put a spoke in your Wheel if I can.	[8]	L'arte schemendo, L'arte adoprando, Di qua pungendo, Di là scherzando, Tutte le macchine Rovescierò.
If you are after A little amusement, You may go dancing, I'll play the tune.		Se vuol ballare, Signor Contino, Il chitarrino Le suonerò.

(Exit.)

Scene Three. *Marcellina and Bartolo. / Recitative*

BARTOLO

But why in Heaven's name Did you wait until this morning To consult me on this matter?	Ed aspettaste il giorno Fissato per le nozze, A parlarmi di questo?

MARCELLINA
(holding a contract in her hand)

I can assure you,	Io non mi perdo,

52

I don't mean to give in yet.
It takes very little
To break off an engagement,
Even later than this time. I've got my contract,
Signed and sealed by Figaro, and I'll see
That he fulfils it. Now then! Our plan must be
To frighten Susanna, make her reject
His lordship's advances, to save her reputation;
Then out of pique against her,
He'll be sure to take my part,
And Figaro will have to marry me then.

Dottor mio, di coraggio:
Per romper de' sponsali
Più avanzati di questo
Bastò spesso un pretesto; ed egli ha meco,

Oltre a questo contratto, certi impegni . . .
So io. Basta: conviene
La Susanna atterrir; convien con arte
Impuntigliarla a rifiutare il Conte.
Egli per vendicarsi
Prenderà il mio partito,
E Figaro così fia mio marito.

BARTOLO
(taking the contract from Marcellina)

Oh well, I'll do what I can, if you will tell me
How the case stands precisely.

Bene, io tutto farò: senza riserve
Tutto a me palesate.

(aside)

'Twould be a good joke
To saddle Figaro with my old Marcellina
Since he once prevented me from marrying Rosina.

Avrei pur gusto
Di dar in moglie la mia serva antica
A chi mi fece un dì rapir l'amica.

No. 4. Aria.

Now for vengeance, ah, now for vengeance!   [9]
Every man of sense enjoys it.
What? Forget so deadly an outrage?
I'm no coward, to stoop so low.

I'll denounce him, I'll confound him,
Like a lawyer I'll get round him,
I'll be even . . . I swear I will, ma'am,
I'm no fool, the man shall know.

La vendetta, oh, la vendetta
È un piacer serbato ai saggi;
L'obliar l'onte, gli oltraggi,
È bassezza, è ognor viltà.

Coll'astuzia, coll'arguzia,
Col giudizio, col criterio
Si potrebbe . . . Il fatto è serio;
Ma, credete, si farà.

Once I can seize on   [10]
The right opportunity,
I shall not let him
Get off with impunity.
I can embarrass him,
Worry him, harrass him;
That is the use of
A knowledge of law.

Se tutto il codice
Dovessi volgere,
Se tutto l'indice
Dovessi leggere,
Con un equivoco,
Con un sinonimo,
Qualche garbuglio
Si troverà.

All Seville knows me,
I'm Doctor Bartolo;
And I'll make Figaro
Learn something more!

Tutta Siviglia
Conosce Bartolo:
Il birbo Figaro
Vinto sarà!

(Exit.)

Scene Four. *Marcellina, then Susanna. / Recitative*

MARCELLINA

I shall not give up hope yet,
If I can win my action.

Tutto ancor non ho perso:
Mi resta la speranza.

(Enter Susanna carrying a cap, a ribbon and a dress.)

(aside)

But here comes Susanna. I'll make a start now,
Pretending not to see her.

Ma Susanna si avanza. Io vo' provarmi . . .
Fingiam di non vederla . . .

(aloud)

So that's the pearl of virtue
He proposes to wed!

È quella buona perla
La vorrebbe sposar!

SUSANNA
(aside, remaining backstage)

That's me she's meaning.

Di me favella.

53

MARCELLINA

That is Figaro all over.	Ma da Figaro, alfine,
Money's all that he cares for: *"l'argent fait tout"*.	Non può meglio sperarsi: *l'argent fait tout*.

SUSANNA
(as before)

Speaks French too. But it's lucky	Che lingua! Manco male
No-one listens to what she says.	Che ognun se quanto vale.

MARCELLINA

Oh yes, she's all discretion,	Brava! questo è giudizio!
So demure in her manners,	Con quegli occhi modesti,
So retiring and modest!	Con quell'aria pietosa,
Besides —	E poi ...

SUSANNA
(as before)

I'd better go.	Meglio è partir.

MARCELLINA

A dear wife she'll make!	Che cara sposa!

Both make as if to leave, and meet in the doorway. / No. 5. Duet

MARCELLINA
(curtseying)

I wish you good day, ma'am,	Via, resti servita,
Your most humble servant!	Madama brillante.

SUSANNA
(curtseying)

Indeed I protest, ma'am,	Non sono si ardita,
Your most humble servant.	Madama piccante.

MARCELLINA
(curtseying again)

'Tis you that go first, ma'am.	No, prima a lei tocca.

SUSANNA
(curtseying again)

No, no, after you.	No, no, tocca a lei.

SUSANNA AND MARCELLINA

I know my good manners,	Io so i dover miei,
I'll not be so rude.	Non fo inciviltà.

MARCELLINA
(as before)

A bride must go first, ma'am.	La sposa novella!

SUSANNA
(as before)

The lady-in-waiting!	La dama d'onore ...

MARCELLINA
(as before)

My lord shows you favour.	Del Conte la bella ...

SUSANNA
(as before)

All Spain favours you, ma'am.	Di Spagna l'amore ...

MARCELLINA

Your quality ...	I meriti ...

SUSANNA

Dignity ...	L'abito ...

MARCELLINA

Position ...	Il posto ...

SUSANNA

Your age!	L'età!

MARCELLINA
(*aside*)

What monstrous impertinence,	Perbacco, precipito,
Take care what you say!	Se ancor resto qua!

SUSANNA
(*aside*)

The shameless old harridan's	Sibilla decrepita!
As good as a play!	Da rider mi fa!

(*Exit Marcellina in fury.*)

Scene Five. *Susanna, then Cherubino. / Recitative*

SUSANNA

Old frump, how I detest her!	Va' là, vecchia pedante,
Treating me like a schoolgirl,	Dottoressa arrogante!
Just because she gave lessons	Perchè hai letto due libri,
To my lady before she ran away.	E seccato Madama in gioventù ...

(*She drapes the dress over the arm-chair.*)

CHERUBINO
(*rushing in*)

Ah, Susanna, you here?	Susannetta, sei tu? ...

SUSANNA

'Tis I. What do you want, Sir?	Son io; cosa volete?

CHERUBINO

Oh, my sweetheart! A misfortune!	Ah, cor mio, che accidente!

SUSANNA

Your sweetheart? What has happened?	Cor vostro? Cosa avvenne?

CHERUBINO

His lordship yesterday	Il Conte, ieri,
Found me all alone with Barbarina,	Perchè trovommi sol con Barbarina,
And dismissed me for ever.	Il congedo mi diede;
And if our gracious lady,	E se la Contessina,
My beautiful godmother,	La mia bella comare,
Cannot get me pardoned, I'm sent away —	Grazia non m'intercede, io vado via,

(*anxiously*)

Never more shall I behold my dear Susanna!	Io non ti vedo più, Susanna mia!

SUSANNA

Never more behold me? Oh dear! And so	Non vedete più me! Bravo! Ma dunque
I was wrong when I imagined	Non più la Contessa
That you were sighing in secret for my lady?	Segretamente il vostro cor sospira?

CHERUBINO

Ah, I only can worship at a distance.	Ah, che troppo rispetto ella m'ispira!
I envy you, who see her	Felice te che puoi
As often as you want to!	Vederla quando vuoi!
You dress her each morning,	Che la vesti il mattino,
At night you undress her, and you fasten	Che la sera la spogli, che le metti
On her brooches and her laces.	Gli spilloni, i merletti ...

(*sighing*)

Ah, were I in your shoes ...	Ah, se in tuo loco ...
What is that you've got there?	Cos'hai lì? dimmi un poco ...

(*imitating him*)

Ah! That's a ribbon belonging to the nightcap
Of my lady your godmother.

Ah, il vago nastro, e la notturna cuffia
Di comare sì bella . . .

CHERUBINO

Oh, give it me, Susanna,
Give it me, I pray.

Deh, dammelo, sorella,
Dammelo, per pietà.

(*He snatches the ribbon from Susanna.*)

SUSANNA

Come, give it me, Sir.

Presto, quel nastro!

(*Susanna tries to take it back, but he runs around the arm-chair.*)

CHERUBINO

The dearest, the sweetest, the luckiest of ribbons!

O caro, o bello, o fortunato nastro!

(*He kisses the ribbon again and again.*)

I'd rather die than give it back.

Io non tel renderò che colla vita.

SUSANNA

(*She chases him, but then stops as if tired.*)

How can you be so naughty?

Cos'è quest'insolenza?

CHERUBINO

Don't be so angry!
A fair exchange, no robbery:
Here's a song I will give you, that I've written.

Eh, via, sta' cheta!
In ricompensa, poi,
Questa mia canzonetta io ti vo' dare.

(*He pulls a song from his pocket.*)

SUSANNA

What use is that to me, pray?

E che ne debbo fare?

(*She takes it from him.*)

CHERUBINO

Sing it, Susanna, sing it!
Sing it before my lady,
Sing it to Barbarina, to Marcellina,

Leggila alla padrona,
Leggila tu medesma,
Leggila a Barbarina, a Marcellina,

(*in transports of ecstasy*)

Sing it to every woman in the castle!

Leggila ad ogni donna del palazzo!

SUSANNA

Poor little Cherubino, are you crazy?

Povero Cherubin, siete voi pazzo?

CHERUBINO

No. 6. Aria

Is it pain, is it pleasure that fills me, [11]
And with feverish ecstasy thrills me?
At the sight of a woman I tremble,
And my heart seems to burst into flame,
My poor heart seems to burst into flame.

Non so più cosa son, cosa faccio . . .
Or di fuoco, ora sono di ghiaccio . . .
Ogni donna cangiar di colore,
Ogni donna mi fa palpitar,
Ogni donna mi fa palpitar.

Love! That word sets me hoping and fearing,
Love! That word that I always am hearing!
Love! Ah love! How can I dissemble
Those desires that I hardly dare name?

Solo ai nomi d'amor, di diletto
Mi si turba, mi s'altera il petto,
E a parlare mi sforza d'amore
Un desio ch'io non posso spiegar!

Only for love I languish,
Dream of delicious anguish!
To every vale and mountain,
To stream, to lake, and fountain,
For love, for love I'm sighing;

Parlo d'amor vegliando,
Parlo d'amor sognando:
All'acque, all'ombre, ai monti,
Ai fiori, all'erbe, ai fonti,
All'eco, all'aria, ai venti

And echo's voice replying Bears back my tender moan . . .	Che il suon de' vani accenti Portano via con sè . . .
And even if none be near me, I talk of love alone, talk of it all alone.	E, se non ho chi m'oda, Parlo d'amor con me.

(*He starts to leave, but sees the Count approaching and returns in terror, hiding behind the arm-chair.*)

Scene Six. *Susanna and Cherubino; later, the Count. / Recitative*

SUSANNA

Quiet, there's someone . . . His lordship! If
  he should find you!
	Taci, vien gente . . . Il Conte! Oh, me
	  meschina!

(She tries to hide Cherubino.)

THE COUNT
(entering)

Susanna, what has happened? You seem all in a flutter.	Susanna, tu mi sembri Agitata e confusa.

SUSANNA
(in confusion)

My lord, I beg your pardon . . . But supposing someone saw you? Think of my reputation!	Signor . . . io chiedo scusa . . . Ma, se mai . . . qui sorpresa . . . Per carità, partite.

COUNT

Just a word, then I leave you. Listen.	Un momento, e ti lascio. Odi.

(He sits on the arm-chair, and takes Susanna's hand; she tears it away.)

SUSANNA

My lord, I cannot.	Non odo nulla.

COUNT

Just one moment! You know The King's appointed me Ambassador to London. That means, of course, That Figaro must go with me.	Due parole. Tu sai Che ambasciatore a Londra Il re mi dichiarò; di condur meco Figaro destinai . . .

SUSANNA
(timidly)

My lord, I beg you . . .	Signor, se osassi . . .

COUNT

Ask me, ask me, my dearest, you know the privilege	Parla, parla, mia cara! E con quel dritto

(standing up)

That you can command. For life I am your servant;	Ch'oggi prendi su me finchè tu vivi,

(tenderly, trying to take her hand again)

What would you? Command me.	Chiedi, imponi, prescrivi.

SUSANNA
(in a frenzy)

My lord, pray let me go; to claim that
  privilege
Is the last thing I wish for. You make me
  wretched.
	Lasciatemi, signor; dritti non prendo:
	Non ne vo', non ne intendo . . . Oh, me
	  infelice!

COUNT

No, no, Susanna, I want to make you happy, For you know how I love you. Did not Basilio Give you my message?	Ah, no, Susanna, io ti vo' far felice! Tu ben sai quanto io t'amo: a te Basilio Tutto già disse.

(trying, as before, to take her hand)

Then listen:	Or senti:

Won't you spare me a moment,
Sometime this evening, and meet me in the
  garden?
Ah, for such a favour you know I'd pay
  you . . .

Se per pochi momenti
Meco in giardin, sull'imbrunir del giorno . . .
Ah, per questo favore io pagherei . . .

BASILIO
(off-stage)

My lord has just gone out.

È uscito poco fa.

COUNT

Who spoke there?

Chi parla?

SUSANNA

Oh heavens!

Oh, Dei!

COUNT

You go, prevent him entering.

Esci, ed alcun non entri.

SUSANNA
(very agitated)

What, and leave you alone here?

Ch'io vi lasci qui solo?

BASILIO
(off-stage)

With my lady perhaps? I'll ask Susanna.

Da Madama sarà: vado a cercarlo.

COUNT
(pointing to the arm-chair)

I'll hide behind this chair.

Qui dietro mi porrò.

SUSANNA

No, don't do that, Sir!

Non vi celate.

COUNT

Quiet! And don't let him stay here!

Taci, e cerca ch'ei parta.

SUSANNA

What next, I wonder?

Ohimè! che fate?

(The Count tries to hide behind the arm-chair, while Susanna places herself between him and the page. The Count pushes her gently back, and she retreats. Meanwhile the page comes round to the front of the arm-chair, jumps into it, and curls up as best he can. Susanna covers him with the dress which she has hung over the arm-chair.)

Scene Seven. *Susanna, Cherubino, the Count, and Basilio. Enter Basilio.*

BASILIO

Susanna, Heaven bless you! I came to ask
If you'd seen his lordship?

Susanna, il ciel vi salvi! Avreste a caso
Veduto il Conte?

SUSANNA

          And what should
I know about his lordship? Pray go away,
  Sir.

         E cosa
Deve far meco il Conte? Animo, uscite.

BASILIO

Wait a moment! I tell you
Figaro wants to find him.

Aspettate, sentite:
Figaro di lui cerca.

SUSANNA
(aside)

     Indeed, Sir?

Oh, cielo!

(to Basilio)

        To find the man
Who hates him as much as you do.

        Ei cerca
Chi dopo voi più l'odia.

I'll hear now how he serves me.	Veggiam come mi serve.

BASILIO

No, you are wrong; it does not always follow	Io non ho mai nella moral sentito
That he who loves a man's wife should hate the lady's husband.	Ch'uno ch'ama la moglie odii il marito.
My lord in fact adores you.	Per dir che il Conte v'ama ...

SUSANNA
(in irritation)

How dare you come to me, Sir,	Sortite, vil ministro
With these vile proposals? I will not listen	Dell'altrui sfrenatezza: io non ho d'uopo
To your talk of his lordship,	Della vostra morale,
His passion, his desires ...	Del Conte, del suo amor ...

BASILIO

Oh, there's no harm done.	Non c'è alcun male.
'Tis a matter of taste, ma'am; yet I confess	Ha ciascun i suoi gusti: io mi credea
I imagined that, like every other woman,	Che preferir doveste per amante,
You would choose for a lover	Come fan tutte quante,
One who's noble, rich, and quite discreet too,	Un signor liberal, prudente e saggio,
Instead of yielding to a pageboy ...	A un giovinastro, a un paggio ...

SUSANNA
(anxiously)

To Cherubino?	A Cherubino!

BASILIO

Yes, Cherubino, *Cherubin d'amore*,	A Cherubino, Cherubin d'amore,
Who earlier this morning	Ch'oggi, sul far del giorno,
Was prowling at your door	Passeggiava qui intorno
Trying to enter ...	Per entrar ...

SUSANNA
(vehemently)

What a slander!	Uom maligno!
All of your own inventing!	Un'impostura è questa!

BASILIO

Is it slander with you to keep one's eyes open?	È un maligno con voi chi ha gli occhi in testa?
And what about that song too?	E quella canzonetta?
Tell me, between ourselves now – I need not tell you	Ditemi in confidenza: io sono amico,
That I never repeat things –	E ad altrui nulla dico:
Was it for you, or for my lady?	È per voi, per Madama?

SUSANNA
(aside, in dismay)

Who the devil's told him that, then?	Chi diavol gliel'ha detto?

BASILIO

A propos, my dear girl,	A proposito, figlia,
'Twould be wiser just to warn him; you've no idea	Istruitelo meglio: egli la guarda
How he gloats upon the Countess	A tavola si spesso,
When he's waiting at table.	E con tale immodestia,
If my lord were to notice – well, need I tell you?	Che s'il Conte s'accorge ... ehi, su tal punto,
On that point he's quite a savage.	Sapete, egli è una bestia.

SUSANNA

Oh, you monster!   Scellerato!
You are always inventing lies   E perchè andate voi
And then spreading them around.   Tai menzogne spargendo?

BASILIO

I? Oh, you wrong me. All I did was to tell Io! che ingiustizia! Quel che compro io
   you   vendo.
What everyone is saying;   A quel che tutti dicono
I've added nothing to it.   Io non aggiungo un pelo.

COUNT
(coming forward)

Well, Sir, what is everyone saying?   Come! che dicon tutti?

BASILIO
(aside)

Delightful!   Oh, bella!

SUSANNA

Oh Heavens!   Oh, cielo!

No. 7. Trio

COUNT
(to Basilio)

How disgraceful! Go at once, Sir! [12]   Cosa sento! Tosto andate,
Find the scoundrel and drive him hence!   E scacciate il seduttor.

BASILIO

My intrusion brought confusion.   [13]   In mal punto son qui giunto!
Pray forgive me, I meant no offence.   Perdonate, o mio signor.

SUSANNA
(half swooning)

Oh, how dreadful! I am ruined,   Che ruina, me meschina!
Faint with terror and suspense.   Son oppressa dal terror.

COUNT AND BASILIO
(helping Susanna)

Ah, poor child, she's almost fainting;   Ah, già svien la poverina!
How her heart beats. What shall we   Come, oddio, le batte il cor!
  do?

BASILIO
(leading her to the arm-chair to seat her in it)

Come, my dear, sit down a moment ...   Pian, pianin: su questo seggio ...

SUSANNA

Ah, where am I?   Dove sono?
         (recovering herself)
    Sir, how dare you?   Cosa veggio?
Let me go, Sir, let me go!   Che insolenza! Andate fuor!
    (She shakes them both off.)

COUNT

Pray be calm and we'll protect you;   Siamo qui per aiutarti,
For your honour is safe you know.   Non turbarti, o mio tesor.

BASILIO
(maliciously)

Pray be calm and we'll protect you;   Siamo qui per aiutarvi:
For your honour is safe you know.   È sicuro il vostro onor.
        (to the Count)
If I mentioned Cherubino   Ah, del paggio quel ch'ho detto
All I said, Sir, was mere conjecture.   Era solo un mio sospetto!

SUSANNA

Sir, I beg you, do not believe him,
What he told you is not true.

È un'insidia, una perfidia:
Non credete all'impostor.

COUNT

I will house the wretch no longer.

Parta! parta, il damerino!

BASILIO AND SUSANNA

Oh, forgive him!

Poverino!

COUNT
(*sarcastically*)

I forgive him?
I know more of him than you.

Poverino!
Ma da me sorpreso ancor.

SUSANNA

How so, Sir? Tell us how.

Come!

BASILIO

What, really? Tell us how.

Che!

Recitative

COUNT

'Twas only yesterday
I chanced to visit Barbarina;
The door was locked, and when she opened
    it
I thought her rather flurried.
This aroused my suspicions;
So I looked in every corner,
    And then gently, gently lifting
    From the table the cloth upon it,
    There was the pageboy!

Da tua cugina
L'uscio ier trovai rinchiuso;
Picchio, m'apre Barbarina
Paurosa fuor dell'uso.
Io dal muso insospettito,
Guardo, cerco in ogni sito,
    Ed alzando pian, pianino
    Il tappeto al tavolino
    Vedo il paggio!

(*He imitates his action with the dress, and discovers the page. In astonishment*)
What, you again, Sir?

Ah, cosa veggio!

SUSANNA
(*fearful*)

I'm lost for ever!

Ah, crude stelle!

BASILIO
(*laughing*)

Ah, how delightful!

Ah, meglio ancora!

COUNT

Oh, you paragon of virtue,
Now I understand it all.

Onestissima signora,
Or capisco come va.

SUSANNA

Everything conspires against me,
Heavens above! What will befall?

Accader non può di peggio:
Giusti Dei! che mai sarà!

BASILIO

Just the same is every woman,
Frail and faithless one and all.

Così fan tutte le belle!
Non c'è alcuna novità.

Recitative

COUNT

Basilio, you go at once and
Tell Figaro to come here.
He'll see himself then . . .

Basilio, in traccia tosto
Di Figaro volate:
Io vo' ch'ei veda . . .

(*Pointing at Cherubino, who remains motionless in his place.*)

SUSANNA
(*gaily*)

And he shall hear too: yes, fetch him.

Ed io che senta: andate.

61

COUNT
(to Basilio)

One moment!   Restate!

(to Susanna)

Are you so brazen? What will you tell him,   Che baldanza! E quale scusa,
When your guilt is so obvious?   Se la colpa è evidente?

SUSANNA

I've done nothing that I need be ashamed   Non ha d'uopo di scusa un'innocente.
   of.

COUNT

When did he come in here then?   Ma costui quando venne?

SUSANNA

         He was already here   Egli era meco
When you made your entrance. He came   Quando voi qui giungeste, e mi chiedea
  to ask me
If I would beg her ladyship   D'impegnar la padrona
To intercede for him; your coming in   A intercedergli grazia: il vostro arrivo
Put us both in confusion,   In scompiglio lo pose,
And he made for the nearest place to hide Ed allor in quel loco si nascose.
  in.

COUNT

But I sat down myself there   Ma s'io stesso m'assisi
As soon as I came into the room!   Quando in camera entrai!

CHERUBINO
(timidly)

I was hiding while you sat there, Sir.   Ed allora di dietro io mi celai.

COUNT

But when I went behind it?   E quando io là mi posi?

CHERUBINO

Then I crept round the chair, and hid   Allor io pian mi volsi, e qui m'ascosi.
  inside it.

COUNT
(to Susanna)

The devil! Then I suppose he's   Oh, ciel! Dunque ha sentito
Heard every word I said to you?   Quello ch'io ti dicea?

CHERUBINO

I did the best I could, Sir, not to listen.   Feci per non sentir quanto potea.

COUNT

Yes, so likely!   Oh, perfidia!

BASILIO

Be careful, Sir, there's someone coming!   Frenatevi: vien gente.

COUNT

And will you sit there still, you little viper? E voi restate qui, picciol serpente!

(He drags him out of the arm-chair.)

Scene Eight. *Susanna, Cherubino, the Count, Basilio, Figaro, peasant men and women.*

Figaro is carrying a white dress in his hand; the peasants carry little baskets of flowers which they scatter in front of the Count. / No. 8. Chorus

CHORUS

Come lads and lasses,   [14]   Giovani liete,
Flowers humbly strewing,   Fiori spargete
And praise with thankful hearts   Davanti al nobile
Our gracious lord.   Nostro signor.

Fairer than all is	Il suo gran core
That flower of virtue	Vi serba intatto
Which to our land of love	D'un più bel fiore
He has restored.	L'almo candor.

Recitative

COUNT
(*to Figaro in astonishment*)

Pray, what is this performance?	Cos'è questa commedia?

FIGARO
(*to Susanna in an undertone*)

Now we're beginning;	Eccoci in danza.
Play up to me, Susanna!	Secondami, cor mio.

SUSANNA
(*aside*)

I fear it's useless.	Non ci ho speranza.

FIGARO
(*to the Count*)

We humbly beg your lordship	Signor, non disdegnate
Graciously to receive us	Questo del nostro affetto
Who have come here to thank you, now you've abolished	Meritato tributo. Or che aboliste
What was once such a pain to honest lovers ...	Un diritto sì ingrato a che ben ama ...

COUNT

That privilege is abolished: what would you further?	Quel dritto or non v'è più: cosa si brama?

FIGARO

We're the first happy couple to obtain	Della vostra saggezza il primo frutto
The advantage of your decree. This very day	Oggi noi coglierem: le nostre nozze
Susanna and I are to be married; so may it please you,	Si son già stabilite. Or a voi tocca
Since by your grace I receive her	Costei, che un vostro dono
As a virtuous bride, to place with your own hands	Illibata serbò, coprir di questa,
Upon her head this symbol of virtue.	Simbolo d'onestà, candida vesta.

COUNT
(*aside*)

That's devilish clever!	Diabolica astuzia!
I'll not be taken in.	Ma fingere convien.

(*aloud*)

My friends, I thank you	Son grato, amici,
For your loyal devotion;	Ad un senso sì onesto.
It was only my duty	Ma non merto, per questo,
To reform these abuses, and I deserve no	Nè tributi nè lodi: e un dritto ingiusto
Praise for having abolished	Ne' miei feudi abolendo,
What offended alike virtue and nature.	A natura, al dover lor dritti io rendo.

ALL

Hurrah for the Lord of the Manor!	Evviva, evviva, evviva!

SUSANNA
(*maliciously*)

Noble words!	Che virtù!

FIGARO

Here is justice!	Che giustizia!

COUNT
(*to Figaro and Susanna*)

And so I promise	A voi prometto

That I'll perform that ceremony. Compier la cerimonia.
I ask your brief indulgence: I purpose that all Chiedo sol breve indugio: io voglio, in faccia
My faithful servants shall see with what splendour De' miei più fidi, e con più ricca pompa,
We'll celebrate your nuptials. Rendervi appien felici.

(aside)

I must find Marcellina. Marcellina si trovi.

(aloud)

Now go, good people. Andate, amici.

CHORUS
(scattering the rest of their flowers)

Come lads and lasses, Giovani liete,
Flowers humbly strewing, Fiori spargete
And praise with thankful hearts Davanti al nobile
Our gracious lord. Nostro signor.

Fairer than all is Il suo gran core
That flower of virtue Vi serba intatto
Which to our land of love D'un più bel fiore
He has restored. L'almo candor.

(Exeunt peasant men and women.)

Recitative

FIGARO

Evviva! Evviva!

SUSANNA

Evviva! Evviva!

BASILIO

Evviva! Evviva!

FIGARO
(to Cherubino)

And where are your good wishes? E voi non applaudite?

SUSANNA

Poor boy, he's so unhappy, È afflitto, poveretto,
Because my lord this morning has dismissed him. Perchè il padron lo scaccia dal castello.

FIGARO

What, on this day of rejoicing? Ah, in un giorno si bello!

SUSANNA

On the day of our wedding! In un giorno di nozze!

FIGARO
(to the Count)

When we all sing your praises! Quando ognuno v'ammira!

CHERUBINO
(kneeling)

Oh, pardon me, my lord! Perdono, mio signor . . .

COUNT

You don't deserve it. Nol meritate.

SUSANNA

He is only a child still. Egli è ancora fanciullo.

COUNT

Not so young as you think him. Men di quel che tu credi.

CHERUBINO

I'm very sorry; of course, I'll never mention . . . È ver, mancai; ma dal mio labbro alfine . . .

64

(raising him from his knees)

Well, well, you shall be pardoned.	Ben, bene; io vi perdono.
Yes, and I'll do still more; there is a place free	Anzi, farò di più; vacante è un posto
For an officer just now in my regiment;	D'uffizial nel reggimento mio;
I give it to you – be off at once now. Good-bye, Sir.	Io scelgo voi. Partite tosto; addio.

(The Count is about to leave, but Susanna and Figaro stop him.)

SUSANNA AND FIGARO

Oh, let him stay for the wedding!	Ah! fin domani sol ...

COUNT

No, he must go now.	No, parta tosto.

CHERUBINO
(sighing with emotion)

I am ready, my lord, and will obey you.	A ubbidirvi, signor, son già disposto.

COUNT

Well, then, for the last time Give Susanna a kiss.	Via, per l'ultima volta La Susanna abbracciate.

(aside)

I took them by surprise then.	Inaspettato è il colpo.

(Exit Count.)

(Cherubino embraces Susanna, who is embarrassed.)

FIGARO

Well, gallant captain, You're forgetting that I'm here.	Ehi, capitano, A me pure la mano.

(softly to Cherubino)

Before you go I've something to tell you.	Io vo' parlarti Pria che tu parta.

(aloud, with assumed gaiety)

Goodbye, goodbye, Master Cherubino. How your destiny changes in one brief moment.	Addio, Picciolo Cherubino. Come cangia in un punto il tuo destino!

No. 9. Aria

Say goodbye now to pastime and play, lad, [15]	Non più andrai, farfallone amoroso,
Say goodbye to your airs and your graces.	Notte e giorno d'intorno girando,
Here's an end to the life that was gay, lad,	Delle belle turbando il riposo,
Here's an end to your games with the girls.	Narcisetto, Adoncino d'amor.
Not for you now are ribbons and laces,	Non più avrai questi bei pennacchini,
Not for you frills and feathers and favours;	Quel cappello leggero e galante,
Pink and white like a girl's though your face is,	Quella chioma, quell'aria brillante,
You must lose all your ringlets and curls.	Quel vermiglio, donnesco color.
Chest thrown out and shoulders back, Sir!	Tra guerrieri, poffar Bacco!
Hold your head up, not so slack, Sir!	Gran mustacchi, stretto sacco,
Take your musket on your shoulder,	Schioppo in spalla, sciabla al fianco,
That's the right style for a soldier,	Collo dritto, muso franco,
Duty calls you to death or glory;	Un gran casco, o un gran turbante,
As to pay, that's another story.	Molto onor, poco contante,
No more dances now, but training	Ed invece del fandango,
For the pleasures of campaigning;	Una marcia per il fango.
Yes, you'll find it quite exciting, [16]	Per montagne, per valloni,
When you come to see some fighting.	Con le nevi e i sollioni,
Bugles calling, sabres flashing,	Al concerto di tromboni,
Cannons roaring, mortars crashing,	Di bombarde, di cannoni,
Headlong into danger dashing –	Che le palle in tutti i tuoni,
Bullets whistling past your ears.	All'orecchio fan fischiar.

Some day you'll come back victorious,
If you don't get killed before;
Then you'll swear that war is glorious,
Oh, a glorious thing is war!

Cherubino, alla vittoria!
Alla gloria militar!
Cherubino, alla vittoria!
Alla gloria militar!

(*Exeunt omnes in military style.*)

Geraint Evans as Figaro with Margaret Marshall as the Countess and Helen Donath as Susanna at Covent Garden, 1980 (photo: Donald Southern)

Act Two

A magnificent room, with an alcove. To the right is the entrance-door, to the left a closet.
At the back a door leading to the servants' rooms. At the side a window.

Scene One. *The Countess alone. / No. 10. Cavatina*

COUNTESS

God of love, I now implore thee, [17]	Porgi, amor, qualche ristoro
Broken-hearted to thee I sigh.	Al mio duolo, a' miei sospir.
Love that once was mine restore me,	O mi rendi il mio tesoro,
Or in mercy let me die.	O mi lascia almen morir.

Scene Two. *The Countess and Susanna; later, Figaro.*

Enter Susanna. / Recitative

Dear Susanna, come here now	Vieni, cara Susanna:
And finish off your story.	Finiscimi l'istoria.

SUSANNA

That's all there is, ma'am.	È già finita.

COUNTESS

So he tried to seduce you?	Dunque, volle sedurti?

SUSANNA

Oh, but his lordship	O, il signor Conte
Does not waste any compliments	Non fa tai complimenti
On a girl of my station;	Con le donne mie pari:
He regards it as purely a matter of business.	Egli venne a contratto di danari.

COUNTESS

Ah, he loves me no longer!	Ah, il crudel più non m'ama!

SUSANNA

Why is he jealous	E come, poi,
If that is the case?	È geloso di voi?

COUNTESS

That is the way now	Come lo sono
Of all modern husbands. They're un-faithful	I moderni mariti: per sistema
On principle, by temperament fickle,	Infedeli, per genio capricciosi,
And only pride gives them cause to be jealous.	E per orgoglio, poi, tutti gelosi,
But if Figaro loves you, you may be certain ...	Ma se Figaro t'ama, ei sol potria ...

FIGARO
(off-stage, humming)

La, la la la, la la la, la la la,	La, la la la, la la la, la la la,
La, la la la, la la la, la.	La, la la la, la la la, la.

(He enters.)

SUSANNA

Here he is. You are wanted;	Eccolo. Vieni, amico:
My lady's quite anxious.	Madama impaziente ...

FIGARO
(gay and self-possessed)

My lady anxious?	A voi non tocca
There is no cause for that, ma'am.	Stare in pena per questo.

'Tis quite a simple matter; his noble lordship
Looks on my bride with favour,
And thinks that he can buy back
In secret that old privilege
Of the Lord of the Manor.
You see it's very possible and very natural.

Alfin, de che si tratta? Al signor Conte
Piace la sposa mia;
Indi segretamente
Ricuperar vorria
Il diritto feudale:
Possibile è la cosa, e naturale.

COUNTESS

Possible?

Possibil!

SUSANNA

Natural?

Natural!

FIGARO

Perfectly natural,
And, if Susanna's willing, perfectly possible.

Naturalissima.
E, se Susanna vuol, possibilissima.

SUSANNA

Have done with all your talking!

Finiscila una volta.

FIGARO

I've done already.
That was why he decided
To take me to London as courier, and choose Susanna
'Confidential attachée to the embassy';
And because she persistently refuses
The diplomatic post which she was offered,
He threatens now to favour Marcellina.
Now you know the whole story.

Ho già finito.
Quindi, prese il partito
Di sceglier me corriero, e la Susanna
Consigliera segreta d'ambasciata:
E, perch'ella ostinata ognor rifiuta
Il diploma d'onor ch'ei le destina,
Minaccia di protegger Marcellina.
Questo è tutto l'affare.

SUSANNA

Have you the heart to speak of this so lightly?
'Tis a serious matter.

Ed hai coraggio di trattar scherzando
Un negozio sì serio?

FIGARO

Aren't you thankful
That I can take it so lightly? Hear what I've done now;

Non vi basta
Che scherzando io ci pensi? Ecco il progetto.

(to the Countess)

I have sent by Basilio
An anonymous letter to warn m'lord
About an assignation
To be given during the ball
To a lover by my lady.

Per Basilio un biglietto
Io gli fo capitar, che l'avvertisca
Di certo appuntamento
Che per l'ora del ballo
A un amante voi deste.

COUNTESS

Oh heavens! How could you?
To a man who's so jealous!

O ciel! che sento!
Ad un uom sì geloso! . . .

FIGARO

So much the better;
That makes it easier still to set him wondering,
To harass him, to embroil him,
To upset all his projects,
To fill him with suspicion, to make him realize
That the game he is playing
Is a game other people can play upon him too.
We'll make him waste all the day in search of the culprit,
And then, all of a sudden, before his noble lordship

Ancora meglio:
Così potrem più presto imbarazzarlo,
Confonderlo, imbrogliarlo,
Rovesciargli i progetti,
Empierlo di sospetti, e porgli in testa
Che la moderna festa,
Ch'ei di fare a me tenta, altri a lui faccia;
Onde qua perda il tempo, ivi la traccia,
Così, quasi *ex abrupto*, e senza ch'abbia

Can interfere with our design,	Fatto per frastornarci alcun disegno,
He will find us married;	Vien l'ora delle nozze,

(to Susanna, pointing to the Countess)

and then I think	in faccia a lei
He'll see that opposition would be useless.	Non fia ch'osi d'opporsi ai voti miei.

SUSANNA

Maybe, but you are reckoning	È ver; ma in di lui vece
Without Marcellina.	S'opporrà Marcellina.

FIGARO
(to Susanna)

One moment – I have it!	Aspetta: al Conte
You'll let his lordship know that he can meet you	Farai subito dir che verso sera
This evening in the garden.	Attendati in giardino:
We'll dress up Cherubino	Il picciol Cherubino,
(I took good care that he should not depart yet),	Per mio consiglio non ancor partito,
Dress him up as a woman,	Da femmina vestito,
And send him to the garden to keep your appointment.	Faremo che in tua vece ivi sen vada.
In the midst of all this	Questa è l'unica strada
My lady arrives, my lord is caught red-handed	Onde Monsù, sorpreso da Madama,
And will thus be completely at her mercy.	Sia costretto a far poi quel che si brama.

COUNTESS
(to Susanna)

Will this do?	Che ti par?

SUSANNA

Pretty well.	Non c'è mal.

COUNTESS

I hope it may then.	Nel nostro caso ...

SUSANNA

When he's once made his mind up ... But is there time now?	Quand'egli è persuaso ... E dove è il tempo? ...

FIGARO

You can just do it nicely; my lord's out hunting,	Ito è il Conte alla caccia, e per qualch'ora
And won't be back for some time yet.	Non sarà di ritorno.

(leaving)

I'll go now and send you	Io vado, e tosto
Cherubino directly; I leave you	Cherubino vi mando: lascio a voi
To look after his disguising.	La cura di vestirlo.

COUNTESS

And then?	E poi?

FIGARO

And then?	E poi ...

Reprise of No. 3.

If my lord's after	Se vuol ballare,
A little amusement,	Signor Contino,
He may go dancing,	Il chitarrino
But I'll play the tune.	Le suonerò.

(Exit.)

Scene Three. *The Countess and Susanna; then Cherubino. / Recitative*

COUNTESS

I'm not happy, Susanna,	Quanto duolmi, Susanna,

To think that Cherubino heard all the things
That his lordship said this morning! Ah! You can't imagine ...
Why did the boy go to you then, Not to me in the first place?
And where's the song he's written?

Che questo giovinetto abbia del Conte
Le stravaganze udite, ah, tu non sai! ...
Ma per qual causa mai
Da me stessa ei non venne? ...
Dov'è la canzonetta?

SUSANNA

Here it is, and when he comes in, We'll make him sing it.
Hush now! who's knocking? I thought so! Come in, come in, Sir!

Eccola: appunto
Facciam che ce la canti.
Zitto, vien gente: è desso. Avanti, avanti,

(Enter Cherubino.)

Forward march, gallant captain!

Signor uffiziale.

CHERUBINO

Oh, do not call me
By such a hateful title! for it reminds me
How soon I must be parted from her,
So kind and gentle –

Ah, non chiamarmi
Con nome si fatale! Ei mi rammenta
Che abbandonar degg'io
Comare tanto buona.

SUSANNA

Yes, and so lovely!

E tanto bella!

CHERUBINO
(sighing)

She is lovely.

Ah ... si ... certo ...

SUSANNA
(imitating him)

She is lovely!

Ah ... si ... certo ...

(aside)

As if you meant it!

Ipocritone!

(aloud)

Make haste, and sing the song now
That you gave me this morning;
Let her ladyship hear it.

Via, presto! La canzone
Che stamane a me deste
A Madama cantate.

COUNTESS
(unfolding it)

Who wrote the song?

Chi n'è l'autor?

SUSANNA
(pointing to Cherubino)

Who wrote it? You need not ask him
When he's blushing all over.

Guardate: egli ha due braccia
Di rossor sulla faccia.

COUNTESS

Take my guitar, Susanna, and play it for him.

Prendi la mia chitarra e l'accompagna.

CHERUBINO

I tremble with emotion,
But if my lady wishes ...

Io sono si tremante ...
Ma se Madama vuole ...

SUSANNA

She does indeed; she does, don't keep her waiting.

Lo vuole, si, lo vuol ... manco parole.

(Susanna plays the refrain on the guitar.) / No. 11. Canzone

Tell me, fair ladies,
Tell me, oh tell,
Has love inspired me?
You know him well.

[18]

Voi che sapete
Che cosa è amor
Donne, vedete
S'io l'ho nel cor.

All that I suffer	Quello ch'io provo
I'll tell you true;	Vi ridirò;
You'll understand it,	È per me nuovo,
I find it new.	Capir nol so.
I feel a longing	Sento un affetto
I can't explain.	Pien di desir
Sometimes a pleasure,	Ch'ora è diletto,
Sometimes a pain.	Ch'ora è martir.
One moment frozen,	Gelo, e poi sento
Then all aflame,	L'alma avvampar,
Then sudden shivering	E in un momento
All through my frame.	Torno a gelar.
Something I'm seeking	Ricerco un bene
Outside of me.	Fuori di me,
Where shall I find it?	Non so chi'l tiene,
What can it be?	Non so cos'è.
Without a reason	Sospiro e gemo
I heave a sigh;	Senza voler,
Sometimes I tremble,	Palpito e tremo
I know not why.	Senza saper,
I know no respite	Non trovo pace
Morning or eve,	Notte nè di:
Yet how delightful	Ma pur mi piace
Thus, thus to grieve.	Languir così.
Tell me, fair ladies,	Voi che sapete
Tell me, oh tell,	Che cosa è amor,
Has love inspired me?	Donne, vedete
You know him well.	S'io l'ho nel cor.

Recitative

COUNTESS

Bravo! Your voice is charming; I never knew that	Bravo! che bella voce! Io non sapea
You could sing so agreeably.	Che cantaste sì bene.

SUSANNA

Oh, as to that,	Oh, in verità
All that he does he's certain to do well.	Egli fa tutto ben quello ch'ei fa.
Come along, gallant captain.	Presto, a noi, bel soldato:
Figaro will have told you ...	Figaro v'informò ...

CHERUBINO

Yes, he has told me.	Tutto mi disse.

SUSANNA

Then let me have a look.	Lasciatemi veder.

(She measures Cherubino against herself.)

Yes, that will be just right –	Andrà benissimo:
We're more or less the same height. Take your coat off.	Siam d'uguale statura ... Già quel manto.

(She takes off his coat.)

COUNTESS

Susanna!	Che fai?

SUSANNA

What is the danger?	Niente paura.

COUNTESS

If someone were to enter –	E se qualcuno entrasse?

SUSANNA

Let them; what harm are we doing?	Entri: che mal facciamo?
But I will lock the door.	La porta chiuderò.

(She closes the door.)

What shall I do now To cover up his hair?	Ma come, poi, Acconciargli i capelli?

COUNTESS

Fetch one of my caps; You will know where to find them. Quickly!	Una mia cuffia Prendi nel gabinetto. Presto!

Susanna goes to the closet to find a cap. Cherubino approaches the Countess, so that she sees the commission which he is clasping to his breast. The Countess takes it and unfolds it, and notices that it has not been sealed.

What is this paper?	Che carta è quella?

CHERUBINO

My commission.	La patente.

COUNTESS

They have not kept you waiting!	Che sollecita gente!

CHERUBINO

'Twas given me by Basilio.	L'ebbi or da Basilio.

COUNTESS

What a hurry! And I see they've forgotten to seal it.	Della fretta obliato hanno il sigillo.

(*She gives it back to him.*)

SUSANNA
(*returning with the cap*)

What is it they've forgotten?	Il sigillo ai che?

COUNTESS

To seal his papers.	Della patente.

SUSANNA

His papers? What already? Here is the cap, ma'am.	Cospetto! Che prematura! Ecco la cuffia.

COUNTESS
(*to Susanna*)

Do be quick. Yes, that's right. If my lord came in now, think what would happen!	Spicciati: va bene. Miserabili noi, se il Conte viene.

SUSANNA
*She takes Cherubino and makes him kneel down in front of her, a little distance away from the Countess, who sits down.** / No. 12. Aria*
[19]

Come here, and kneel immediately, Keep quiet if you can;	Venite ... inginocchiatevi ... Restate fermo lì ...

(*She combs his hair on one side; then she takes him by the chin and turns his head about as she wishes.*)

And now just turn your face away, Bravo, that suits my plan.	Pian piano, or via, giratevi ... Bravo ... va ben così.
Come, turn full face towards me now,	La faccia ora volgetemi,

(*While Susanna is arranging his hair, Cherubino gazes tenderly at the Countess.*)

To me, over there! Look straight at me, I tell you, Sir! My lady is not there.	Olà! quegli occhi a me ... Drittissimo ... guardatemi ... Madama qui non è.

(*She carries on doing his hair and holds out the cap to him.*)

Turn down your collar neatly, To fold your hands before you, Remember when you're walking,	Più alto quel colletto ... Quel ciglio un po' più basso ... Le mani sotto il petto ...

---

* Mozart replaced this aria with the *Arietta 'Un moto di gioia'* for the 1789 revival of the opera, when Adriana del Bene sang Susanna.

To look discreetly downwards.	Vedremo poscia il passo,
Now let me see you try.	Quando sarete in piè.

(softly to the Countess)

Just look at him, my lady!	Mirate il bricconcello,
We'll put him through his paces.	Mirate quanto è bello!
Where did he get those glances?	Che furba guardatura,
Such naughty airs and graces?	Che vezzo, che figura!
If women all go mad for him,	[20] Se l'amano le femmine,
They have good reason why.	Han certo il lor perchè.

COUNTESS

Really, you are too silly.	Quante buffonerie!

SUSANNA

I'm half afraid	Ma se ne sono
I am going to be jealous!	Io medesma gelosa!

(She takes Cherubino by the chin.)

You little mischief,	Ehi, serpentello,
How dare you have the face to be so pretty?	Volete tralasciar d'esser sì bello?

COUNTESS

Susanna, no more nonsense! I think you'll have to pull up	Finiam le ragazzate. Or quelle maniche
His sleeves to the elbow;	Oltre il gomito gli alza,
Then they will not be in the way	Onde più agiatamente
When you put his dress on.	L'abito gli si adatti.

SUSANNA

(carrying out her instructions)

There now!	Ecco.

COUNTESS

Still higher!	Più indietro.
That's right.	Così ...

(She finds a ribbon tied around his arm.)

What is that ribbon?	Che nastro è quello?

SUSANNA

Ah, that is stolen property!	È quel ch'esso involommi.

COUNTESS

(untying the ribbon)

And stained with blood too!	E questo sangue?

CHERUBINO

(agitated)

I don't know how it happened,	Quel sangue ... Io non so come ...
Just now I tripped over	Poco pria, sdrucciolando
Onto a stone. I bruised my arm a little	In un sasso ... le pelle io mi sgraffiai,
And I bound it with this to stop the bleeding.	E la piaga col nastro io mi fasciai.

SUSANNA

Let me see! Nothing much. Look there now! His arm is	Mostrate: non è mal. Cospetto! Ha il braccio
Much whiter than my own is; many a girl now ...	Più candido del mio! Qualche ragazza ...

COUNTESS

You talk too much Susanna!	E segui a far la pazza?
Go and look in the dressing-room, you'll find the English	Va' nel mio gabinetto, e prendi un poco
Taffeta there; it's in my cupboard.	D'inglese taffetà, ch'è sullo scrigno.

(Exit Susanna hurriedly.)

About this ribbon –	In quanto al nastro ...

(She examines her ribbon briefly. Cherubino kneels before her and watches her closely.)

I think I'd like to keep it;	... inver ... per il colore ...
It's a colour that suits me.	Mi spiacea di privarmene ...

SUSANNA
(coming back and giving her the taffeta and scissors)

Some taffeta,
And we shall want a bandage.

Tenete:
E da legarli il braccio?

COUNTESS

Then, as you're going,
Fetch another piece of ribbon.

Un altro nastro
Prendi insiem col mio vestito.

(Exit Susanna by the rear door taking Cherubino's coat with her.)

CHERUBINO

No, 'tis that piece that alone could have
healed me.

Ah, più presto m'avria quello guarito!

COUNTESS

But why? Must it be this one?

Perchè? Questo è migliore.

CHERUBINO

But if a ribbon
Has bound the hair, or touched the hair of
someone ...
Some person ...

Allorchè un nastro
Legò la chioma, ovver toccò la pelle ...

D'oggetto ...

COUNTESS
(interrupting him)

... Who's a stranger,
It has the power of healing! Do you think
so?
I did not know such qualities existed.

... Forestiero,
È buon per le ferite; non è vero?

Guardate qualità ch'io non sapea!

CHERUBINO

My lady mocks me, when I am forced to
leave her.

Madama scherza, ed io frattanto parto.

COUNTESS

'Tis indeed a misfortune.

Poverin, che sventura!

CHERUBINO

How can I bear it?

Oh, me infelice!

COUNTESS
(moved and agitated)

You're crying?

Or piange!

CHERUBINO

Indeed I wish that I could die now!
Then at the last, when all was nearly over,
These my lips might entreat you ...

O ciel! perchè morir non lice!
Forse, vicino all'ultimo momento ...
Questa bocca oseria ...

COUNTESS

Cherubino, what nonsense you are talking!
Oh, who can that be knocking?

Siate saggio: cos'è questa follia?

(She dries his eyes with her handkerchief. There is a knock at the door.)
Chi picchia alla mia porta?

Scene Four. *The Countess, Cherubino; with the Count off-stage behind the door.*

COUNT
(off-stage)

Why's the door locked?

Perchè chiusa?

COUNTESS
(standing up)

'Tis my husband! Oh, heavens, I'm lost
now!

Il mio sposo! O Dei, son morta!

(to Cherubino)

You here, without your coat on,	Voi qui senza mantello,
Looking like this too! He will have had that letter . . .	In questo stato! Un ricevuto foglio . . .
And he's always so jealous . . .	La sua gran gelosia!

COUNT
(louder)

Why don't you open?	Cosa indugiate?

COUNTESS
(in confusion)

I'm alone here, really alone here!	Son sola . . . ah, si, son sola . . .

COUNT

I heard you talking.	E a chi parlate?

COUNTESS

I, talking? Was I? 'Twas with you then.	A voi . . . certo . . . A voi stesso . . .

CHERUBINO

After all that has happened, he'll be so angry,	Dopo quel ch'è successo, il suo furore . . .
I dare not let him find me.	Non trovo altro consiglio!

(He goes into the closet and shuts the door.)

COUNTESS

Heaven alone can save me in this danger.	Ah, mi difenda il cielo, in tal periglio!

(She takes the key from the closet door and runs to open the door for the Count.)

Scene Five. *The Countess, and the Count in hunting dress.*

COUNT
(entering)

What does this mean? It is rather unusual	Che novità! Non fu mai vostra usanza
To find your door locked.	Di rinchiudervi in stanza!

COUNTESS

It is, but I was . . .	È ver; ma io . . .
I mean, I was just trying . . .	Io stava qui mettendo . . .

COUNT

You were trying . . .	Via: mettendo . . .

COUNTESS

A new dress on, there was no-one but Susanna;	Certe robe . . . Era meco la Susanna . . .
She has gone to her room now.	Che in sua camera è andata.

COUNT
(looking at her closely)

In any case	Ad ogni modo,
You seem disturbed about something.	Voi non siete tranquilla.
Pray, Madam, read this letter.	Guardate questo foglio.

(giving her a letter)

COUNTESS
(aside)

Heavens! 'Tis Figaro's	Numi! È il foglio
Anonymous letter.	Che Figaro gli scrisse!

(Cherubino knocks over a chair and writing-table in the closet, making a loud noise.)

COUNT

What's making all that noise in there?	Cos'è codesto strepito?
I think that something's	In gabinetto
Fallen down in your dressing-room.	Qualche cosa è caduta.

COUNTESS

Really, I heard nothing.

Io non intesi niente.

COUNT

Then you must be very preoccupied indeed, Ma'am.

Convien che abbiate i gran pensieri in mente.

COUNTESS

Am I?

Di che?

COUNT

Someone's inside there.

Là v'è qualcuno.

COUNTESS

Who do you think it is then?

Chi volete che sia?

COUNT

You can tell me that.
I've only just come in here.

Lo chiedo a voi ...
Io vengo in questo punto.

COUNTESS

Ah, yes, Susanna, of course ...

Ah, sì, Susanna ... appunto ...

COUNT

But you told me Susanna went to her own room.

Che passò, mi diceste, alla sua stanza!

COUNTESS

Either to her room, or mine, I did not notice.

Alla sua stanza, o qui: non vidi bene ...

COUNT

In that case, what is the reason I find you so perturbed, Ma'am?

Susanna! E donde viene
Che siete sì turbata?

COUNTESS
(forcing a little laugh)

On account of my maid?

Per la mia cameriera?

COUNT

That's as it may be;
Anyway, you're perturbed, Ma'am.

Io non so nulla:
Ma turbata, senz'altro.

COUNTESS

I think it's you, my lord,
Who is so perturbed about my maid.

Ah! questa serva,
Più che non turba me, turba voi stesso.

COUNT

Perhaps you're right, Ma'am, and I will show you the reason.

È vero, è vero; e lo vedrete adesso.

Scene Six. *The Countess, the Count. Susanna on one side.*

Enter Susanna by the door by which she left. She stops when she sees the Count speaking at the closet door. / No. 13. Trio

COUNT

Come out, come out, Susanna,
Come out at once, I say!

[21] Susanna, or via, sortite,
Sortite! Così vo'.

COUNTESS

No, no, my lord, have patience;
She can't your word obey.

Fermatevi ... Sentite ...
Sortire ella non può.

SUSANNA
(*aside*)

Oh, where is Cherubino?
How did he get away?

Cos'è codesta lite?
Il paggio dove andò?

76

COUNT

Why can't she then obey me?	E chi vietarlo or osa?

COUNTESS

For shame, Sir! Decency!	Lo vieta l'onestà:
She's gone into my chamber,	Un abito da sposa
Her wedding-dress to try.	Provando ella si sta.

COUNT
(aside)

'Tis all too plain the reason;	Chiarissima è la cosa:
A man's in there I know.	L'amante qui sarà!

COUNTESS
(aside)

Too horrible this moment.	Bruttissima è la cosa:
Whatever shall I do?	Chi sa cosa sarà.

SUSANNA
(aside)

Ah! Now I understand it;	Capisco qualche cosa:
We'll see how things will go.	Veggiamo come va.

COUNT

Well let me hear your voice then,	Dunque, parlate almeno,
Susanna, if you are there!	Susanna, se qui siete . . .

COUNTESS

No, no, no, do not answer;	Nemmen, nemmen, nemmeno!
(towards the door)	
I order you be silent!	Io v'ordino, tacete!

SUSANNA
(aside, hiding in the alcove)

Oh, what a situation!	O cielo! Un precipizio,
A scandal such as never was	Un scandalo, un disordine
Will come of this, I know.	Qui certo nascerà.

COUNT AND COUNTESS

And you, my lord, } be careful!	Consorte { mia, giudizio!
My lady, pray, }	{ mio,
A scandal such as never was	Un scandalo, un disordine
Will come of this, I know!	Schiviam, per carità.

Recitative

COUNT

You'll not unlock the door, Ma'am?	Dunque, voi non aprite?

COUNTESS

And pray, why should I	E perchè deggio
When the room is my own?	Le mie camere aprir?

COUNT

Just as it suits you;	Ebben, lasciate . . .
Then I'll have it forced open. Ho, you there!	L'aprirem senza chiavi . . . Ehi gente! . . .

COUNTESS

What, Sir?	Come?
Do you propose to question	Porreste a repentaglio
My honour in public?	D'una dama l'onore?

COUNT

I was hasty, I grant you.	È vero, io sbaglio.
It shall all be done quietly.	Posso, senza rumore,
We must not have a scandal before the servants.	Senza scandalo alcun di nostra gente,
I'll go myself now and fetch the tools to do it.	Andar io stesso a prender l'occorrente:

You will please to wait here, Ma'am; no 'twill be better,	Attendete pur qui . . . Ma, perchè in tutto
To prevent all collusion, I will lock the other Entrance to this room.	Sia il mio dubbio distrutto, anco le porte Io prima chiuderò.

(*He locks the door leading to the maids' rooms.*)

COUNTESS
(*aside*)

What will happen?	Che imprudenza!

COUNT

And I desire that you too Will have the goodness to come with me.	Voi la condiscendenza Di venir meco avrete.

(*putting on a show of gaiety*)

Allow me to offer you my arm, Ma'am.	Madama, eccovi il braccio. Andiamo.

COUNTESS
(*trembling*)

Your servant!	Andiamo.

COUNT
(*in a loud voice, pointing to the closet.*)

Susanna will stay there till I release her.	Susanna starà qui finchè torniamo.

(*Exeunt.*)

Scene Seven. *Susanna and Cherubino. / No. 14. Duet*

SUSANNA
(*coming out of the alcove hurriedly and going to the closet door*)

Be quick, unlock the door now,	[22]	Aprite, presto, aprite!
It's only me, Susanna.		Aprite: è la Susanna.
Come quickly, oh, come quickly		Sortite, via, sortite, . . .
No longer must you stay.		Andate via di qua!

CHERUBINO
(*entering breathless and in confusion*)

Susanna, 'tis too terrible.	Ahimè, che scena orribile!
Do help me now, I pray.	Che gran fatalità!

(*They go first to one door, then to another, and find them all locked.*)

SUSANNA

Come here, go there, go there!	Di qua, di qua, di là.

SUSANNA AND CHERUBINO

The doors are locked and bolted.	Le porte son serrate.
What shall we do to find a way?	Che mai, che mai sarà!

CHERUBINO

I'm lost if I stay longer.	Qui perdersi non giova.

SUSANNA

He'll kill you if he finds you.	V'uccide, se vi trova.

CHERUBINO

Then I must try the window.	Veggiamo un po' qui fuori.

(*standing by the window which gives onto the garden*)

It looks into the garden.	Dà proprio nel giardino.

(*He makes as if to jump out, but Susanna holds him back.*)

SUSANNA

Not that way, Cherubino.	Fermate, Cherubino!

(*She looks out, then draws back.*)

Be careful, do not try!	Fermate, per pietà!

CHERUBINO

Just underneath are flowers,	Qui perdersi non giova:
It isn't very high.	M'uccide, se mi trova.

SUSANNA

(still holding him back)

You'll break your neck for certain,	Tropp'alto, per un salto.
Be careful, do not try!	Fermate, per pietà!

CHERUBINO

(breaking away from Susanna)

What of that? Ere I injure her,	Lasciami: pria di nuocerle,
I'd leap into a fire.	Nel foco volerei.
She is my heart's desire . . .	Abbraccio te per lei,
So kiss and say goodbye.	Addio. Così si fa.

SUSANNA

He'll break his neck for certain,	Ei va a perire, oh, Dei!
Not that way, 'tis too high!	Fermate, per pietà.

Cherubino jumps out; Susanna gives a loud cry, sits down for a moment, then goes to the window / Recitative

Look at the little rascal, how he's running!	Oh, guarda il demonietto! Come fugge!
He's a mile off already.	È già un miglio lontano!
No time for me to lose now;	Ma non perdiamci invano.
I'll slip into the dressing-room.	Entriam nel gabinetto:
Pray, come in, jealous husband! I'm ready for you.	Venga poi lo smargiasso, io qui l'aspetto.

(She goes into the closet and shuts the door behind her.)

Scene Eight. *The Count and Countess.*

(Re-enter the Count and Countess, the former carrying a hammer and pliers in his hand. As soon as he enters, he examines all the doors, etc.)

COUNT

All is just as I left it. Now, are you willing	Tutto è come il lasciai: colete dunque
To unlock the door . . .	Aprir voi stessa . . .

(about to force the door open)

or must I . . .	o deggio . . .

COUNTESS

Stay, I beseech you,	Ahimè, fermate,
Do but hear me a moment.	E ascoltatemi un poco.

(The Count throws the hammer and pliers onto a chair.)

Do you mean that you really	Mi credete capace
Could believe me untrue?	Di mancare al dover? . . .

COUNT

Just as you please, Ma'am.	Come vi piace.
I mean to see this instant	Entro quel gabinetto
Who is locked in that room.	Chi v'è chiuso vedrò.

COUNTESS

(in fear and trembling)

Yes, you shall see him . . .	Sì, lo vedrete . . .
But do be calm and listen.	Ma uditemi tranquillo.

COUNT

(angrily)

Then it is not Susanna?	Non è dunque Susanna!

COUNTESS

(as before)

No, there's somebody else there,	No, ma invece è un oggetto
One whose harmless intentions	Che ragion di sospetto
You've no right to suspect. I was preparing	Non vi deve lasciar: per questa sera . . .
For this evening's amusement	Una burla innocente
A harmless piece of fooling, and I will swear to you	Di far si disponeva . . . ed io vi giuro . . .
That my truth . . . and my honour . . .	Che l'onor . . . l'onestà . . .

79

COUNT
(*angrier still*)

Who is it? Tell me!   Chi è dunque? Dite! . . .
I'll have his blood!   L'ucciderò.

COUNTESS

Oh, listen!   Sentite.
I cannot speak.   Ah, non ho cor.

COUNT

I'm listening.   Parlate.

COUNTESS

He's a child.   È un fanciullo . . .

COUNT
(*as before*)

He's a child?   Un fanciul . . .

COUNTESS

Yes, Cherubino.   Sì, Cherubino.

COUNT
(*beside himself*)

Am I condemned to find him   E mi farà il destino
Everywhere that I turn, this imp of   Ritrovar questo paggio in ogni loco!
mischief?

(*to the Countess*)

What's this? Hasn't he gone yet! All is clear   Come? non è partito? Scellerati!
now.
This explains your confusion, all my   Ecco i dubbi spiegati, ecco l'imbroglio,
suspicions.
Now I can understand that anonymous   Ecco il raggiro onde m'avverte il foglio.
letter!

No. 15. / Finale

COUNT
(*at the closet door, in a rage*)

Out you come, no more concealment,   [23]   Esci, omai, garzon malnato!
Out you come, then out you go!   Sciagurato, non tardar.

COUNTESS

Do not hurt him, I beseech you,   Ah, signore, quel furore
(*dragging the Count back*)
He is innocent, you know.   Per lui fammi il cor tremar.

COUNT

Would you still be interfering?   E d'opporvi ancor osate?

COUNTESS

No, but hear me . . .   No, sentite . . .

COUNT

Well, go on then.   Via, parlate.

COUNTESS
(*trembling in terror*)

He is innocent, I swear it!   Giuro al ciel ch'ogni sospetto . . .
When you see him, oh, don't be angry,   E lo stato in che il trovate . . .
In his shirt-sleeves, without a collar.   Sciolto il collo . . . nudo il petto . . .

COUNT

In his shirt-sleeves . . .   Sciolto il collo . . .
Without a collar . . . Yes, go on then.   Nudo il petto . . . Seguitate.

COUNTESS

'Twas to dress him as a lady . . .   Per vestir femminee spoglie . . .

80

COUNT

Dressing up, indeed, my lady!
I'll give him a dressing down.

Ah, comprendo, indegna moglie;
Mi vo' tosto vendicar!

(He approaches the closet, then turns back.)

COUNTESS
(forcefully)

Oh, my lord, you are too cruel,
How far will you drag me down?

Mi fa torto, quel trasporto;
M'oltraggiate, a dubitar.

COUNT

Where's that key, Ma'am?

Qua la chiave.

COUNTESS

No, he is blameless,
Let me tell you . . .

Egli è innocente,
Voi sapete . . .

(She hands the Count the key.)

COUNT

Tell me nothing!
Go, from henceforth I renounce you!
And as faithless I denounce you!
Go, forever hide your shame,
You've disgraced my house and name.

Non so niente.
Va' lontan dagli occhi miei.
Un'infida, un'empia sei . . .
E mi cerchi d'infamar.

COUNTESS

Banished? Yes . . . but . . .

Vado . . . sì . . . ma . . .

COUNT

No, I'll not hear you.

Non ascolto.

COUNTESS

But I am guiltless!

Non son rea . . .

COUNT

Your eyes accuse you!
I'll have vengeance on this traitor!   [24]
Yes, for this I'll make him bleed.

Vel leggo in volto.
Mora, mora, e più non sia
Ria cagion del mio penar!

COUNTESS

Ah, how blind his jealous passion!
'Twill provoke some fatal deed.

Ah, la cieca gelosia
Qualche eccesso gli fa far! . . .

(The Count opens the closet door, and Susanna comes forward with a straight face, and stops at the door.)

Scene Nine. *The Countess, the Count and Susanna.*

COUNT
(in astonishment)

Susanna!

Susanna!

COUNTESS
(in astonishment)

Susanna!

Susanna!

SUSANNA

Your servant!   [25]
But why this amazement?

Signore!
Cos'è quel stupore?

(ironically)

If you're still intending
To kill Cherubino,
You see him before you,
The traitor . . . 'twas me!

Il brando prendete,
Il paggio uccidete;
Quel paggio malnato
Vedetelo qua.

COUNT
(aside)

I'm baffled, confounded,
Some trick here I see.

Che scuola! La testa
Girando mi va.

81

COUNTESS
(aside)

I can't understand it,
The boy, where is he?

Che storia è mai questa!
Susanna v'è là?

SUSANNA

So rare a confusion
I never did see.

Confusa han la testa:
Non san come va.

COUNT
(to Susanna)

He's there still.

Sei sola? ...

SUSANNA
(to the Count)

Pray, look, Sir,
And find what you can.

Guardate,
Qui ascoso sarà.

COUNT

He's there still, I know it,
I'll soon find my man.

Guardiamo, guardiamo,
Qui ascoso sarà.

(He goes into the closet.)

COUNTESS

Susanna, I'm breathless,
With terror I'm fainting.

Susanna, son morta:
Il fiato mi manca.

SUSANNA
(with great gaiety pointing to the window from which Cherubino jumped)

The boy's out of danger;
Take heart, ma'am, I pray.

Più lieta, più franca!
In salvo è di già.

COUNT
(coming out of the closet in confusion)

I can't find a soul there,
And yet I was certain.
I wronged you, my lady,
I ask your forgiveness.
But was not such trickery
Too cruel for play?

Che sbaglio mai presi!
Appena lo credo.
Se a torto v'offesi,
Perdono vi chiedo;
Ma far burla simile
È poi crudeltà.

COUNTESS AND SUSANNA
(The Countess holds her handkerchief to her mouth to conceal her emotions.)

'Tis you that for cruelty
Now have to pay.

Le vostre follie
Non mertan pietà.

COUNT

My dearest!

Io v'amo!

COUNTESS
(gradually recovering from her confusion)

No, no, Sir.

Nol dite!

COUNT

I love you!

Vel giuro!

COUNTESS
(forcefully and angrily)

Not so, Sir.
You swore you'd renounce me,
As faithless denounce me.

Mentite!
Son l'empia, l'infida
Che ognora v'inganna.

COUNT

Oh, help me, Susanna,
Oh, what can I say?

Quell'ira, Susanna,
M'aita a calmar.

82

To doubt and suspicion You should not give way; Let this be a warning To you from today.	Così si condanna Chi può sospettar, Così si condanna Chi può sospettar.

COUNTESS
(with resentment)

For years of devotion So patient and faithful, Shall I be rewarded With doubt and dismay?	Adunque la fede D'un'anima amante, Sì fiera mercede Doveva sperar?

COUNT

Oh, help me, Susanna, Oh, what can I say?	Quell'ira, Susanna, M'aita a calmar.

SUSANNA
(having repeated her previous verses to the Count, turns to the Countess with a beseeching gesture)

My lady!	Signora!

COUNT
(in a beseeching attitude)

Rosina!	Rosina!

COUNTESS
(to the Count)

How cruel! Rosina no longer, But now sad and lonely, A woman deserted, And you take pleasure In causing her pain.	Crudele! Più quella non sono, Ma il misero oggetto Del vostro abbandono, Che avete diletto Di far disperar.

COUNT AND SUSANNA

Forgive { him, dear Madam. { me, I pray you. Enough { he's been banished, { have I suffered, I'm sure } that { he will never doubt you again. I swear } { I	Confuso, pentito, Son } troppo punito: È } Abbiate pietà.

COUNTESS

Ungrateful! Then from all suspicion You must now refrain.	Crudele! Soffrir sì gran torto Quest' alma non sa.

COUNT

The boy was not here then?...	Ma il paggio rinchiuso?...

COUNTESS

'Twas only to tease you.	Fu sol per provarvi.

COUNT

Your trembling anxiety...	Ma i tremiti, i palpiti?...

COUNTESS

All jesting, so please you!	Fu solo per burlarvi.

COUNT

But what does this letter mean?	Ma un foglio sì barbaro?...

COUNTESS AND SUSANNA

The writer was Figaro, The bearer Basilio...	Di Figaro è il foglio, E a voi, per Basilio...

COUNT

I'll punish the rascals...	Ah, perfidi! Io voglio...

No! No, 'tis enough,
Let us live and let live.

Perdono non merta
Chi agli altri nol dà.

COUNT
(*tenderly*)

Well then, to oblige you
Let all be forgotten.
Rosina, how can you be
So cruel to me?

Ebben, se vi piace,
Comune è la pace:
Rosina inflessibile
Con me non sarà.

COUNTESS

You know me, Susanna,
I can't help forgiving;
What woman could ever
So hard-hearted be?

Ah, quanto, Susanna,
Son dolce di core!
Di donna al furore
Chi più crederà?

SUSANNA

'Tis always the same, ma'am,
When husbands have wronged us,
They know how to trade
On our weakness, you see.

Cogli uomin, signora,
Girate, volgete,
Vedrete che ognora
Si cade poi là.

COUNT
(*tenderly*)

Oh look at me!

Guardatemi . . .

COUNTESS

For shame, Sir!

Ingrato!

COUNT

I've wronged you, and repent it.

Ho torto, e mi pento!

(*He kisses the Countess's hand over and over again.*)

COUNT, COUNTESS AND SUSANNA

And now all is over,
Was ever a husband
So jealous and blind?
Was ever a wife
So devoted and kind?

Da questo momento

Quest'alma a conoscer $\left\{\begin{array}{l}\text{vi}\\\text{mi}\\\text{la}\end{array}\right.$

Apprender potrà.

Scene Ten. *The Count, Countess, Susanna and Figaro*

FIGARO
(*entering*)

My lord and my lady,
The music is ready;
The trumpets are braying,
The pipers are playing,
With dancing and singing,
And bells all a-ringing,
They come to salute us
As bridegroom and bride.

[26]

Signori, di fuori
Son già i suonatori;
Le trombe sentite,
I pifferi udite.
Tra canti, tra balli
De' vostri vassalli,
Corriamo, voliamo
Le nozze a compir!

(*He takes Susanna's arm and makes as if to leave; the Count holds him back.*)

COUNT

No, no, not so fast, Sir.

Pian piano, men fretta.

FIGARO

The people are waiting . . .

La turba m'aspetta.

COUNT

One thing I must know which
Perhaps you can tell.

Un dubbio toglietemi
In pria di partir.

What new danger's coming?	La cosa è scabrosa;
You never can tell!	Com'ha da finir?
Now I must be careful	Con arte le carte
And play my cards well.	Convien qui scoprir.

COUNT

(Showing him the letter from Basilio; Figaro pretends to examine it.)

Here's a letter, master Figaro,	[27] Conoscete, signor Figaro,
Have you seen it once before?	Questo foglio chi vergò?

FIGARO

I have not, Sir.	Nol conosco ...

SUSANNA
(to Figaro)

Never seen it?	Nol conosci?

FIGARO

No.	No.

COUNTESS
(to Figaro)

Never seen it?	Nol conosci?

FIGARO

No.	No.

COUNT
(to Figaro)

Never seen it?	Nol conosci?

FIGARO

No.	No.

COUNT, COUNTESS AND SUSANNA

Never seen it?	Nol conosci?

FIGARO

No, no, no!	No, no, no!

SUSANNA

Never gave it to Basilio ...	E nol desti a Don Basilio ...

COUNTESS

To deliver ...	Per recarlo ...

COUNT

You remember ...	Tu c'intendi ...

FIGARO

Not I, no, no!	Oibò, oibò.

SUSANNA

Nor about the assignation ...	E non sai del damerino ...

COUNTESS

For this evening, in the garden ...	Che stasera, nel giardino ...

COUNT

Don't you know now ...	Già capisci ...

FIGARO

Not I, no, no.	Non lo so.

COUNT

'Tis no good to make excuses,	Cerchi invan difesa e scusa.
In your face I read the truth, Sir,	Il tuo ceffo già t'accusa;
I can see you've told a lie.	Veggo ben che vuoi mentir.

FIGARO
(to the Count)

Then my face, Sir, is the liar.	Mente il ceffo, io già non mento.

COUNTESS AND SUSANNA
(to Figaro)

All your cunning's waste of labour,	Il talento aguzzi invano.
For we've told my lord the secret.	Palesato abbiam l'arcano:
'Tis too late now to deny.	Non v'è nulla da ridir.

COUNT

Well, your answer?	Che rispondi?

FIGARO

I have none, Sir!	Niente, niente.

COUNT

Then you own it?	Dunque, accordi?

FIGARO

No, I don't, Sir!	Non accordo.

COUNTESS AND SUSANNA
(to Figaro)

Hold your tongue, you silly fellow,	Eh, via chetati, balordo:
Now this comedy must end.	La burletta ha da finir.

FIGARO

Then to have a happy ending	Per finirla lietamente
In theatrical tradition,	E all'usanza teatrale,

(taking Susanna's arm)

By your lordship's kind permission	Un'azion matrimoniale
To be married we intend.	Le faremo ora seguir.

SUSANNA, FIGARO AND COUNTESS
(to the Count)

Grant us now, my lord, your favour,	Deh, signor, nol contrastate:
Pray no longer bar the way,	Consolate i $\begin{cases} \text{miei} \\ \text{lor} \end{cases}$ desir.
And let nothing spoil our pleasure	Deh, signor, nol contrastate,
On our happy wedding day.	Consolate i $\begin{cases} \text{miei} \\ \text{lor} \end{cases}$ desir.

COUNT
(aside)

Where's that woman Marcellina?	Marcellina, Marcellina,
What's the cause of her delay?	Quanto tardi a comparir!

Scene Eleven. *The Count, Countess, Susanna, Figaro and Antonio.*
(Enter Antonio, the gardener, half drunk, carrying a pot of flattened carnations/geraniums.)

ANTONIO
(in fury)

Oh, my lord! . . . my lord! . . .	Ah! signore . . . signor . . .

COUNT
(anxiously)

What's the matter?	Cosa è stato?

ANTONIO

Oh, my lord, oh, my lady, look here!	Che insolenza! Ch'il fece, chi fu?

COUNT, COUNTESS, FIGARO AND SUSANNA
(anxiously)

What is all this about? What has happened?	Cosa dici, cos'hai, cosa è nato?

ANTONIO

Just you listen!	Ascoltate.

86

COUNT, COUNTESS, FIGARO AND SUSANNA

Go on, let us hear!　　　　　　　　　Via, parla, di' su.

ANTONIO

Every day from the window they throw down　　Dal balcone che guarda in giardino
All their rubbish and muck to the garden　　Mille cose ogni di gittar veggio;
But 'twas never so bad as today, Sir!　　E poc'anzi, può darsi di peggio?
For just now they have thrown out a man!　　Vidi un uom, signor mio, gittar giù!

COUNT
(*alertly*)

From that window?　　　　　　　　　Dal balcone?

ANTONIO
(*pointing to the broken flowerpot*)

And smashed my geraniums.　　　　　Vedete i garofani?

COUNT

In the garden?　　　　　　　　　　In giardino?

ANTONIO

Yes!　　　　　　　　　　　　　　Si!

SUSANNA AND COUNTESS
(*in an undertone to Figaro*)

Now you must help us!　　　　　　Figaro, all'erta!

COUNT

What can this mean?　　　　　　　Cosa sento!

COUNTESS, SUSANNA AND FIGARO
(*aside*)

'Tis most inconvenient;　　　　　　Costui ci sconcerta.
(*aloud*)
Who allowed this old drunkard in here?　　Quel briaco che viene a far qui?

COUNT
(*excitedly, to Antonio*)

But the man that you saw, where is he now?　　Dunque un uom ... Ma dov'è, dov'è gito?

ANTONIO

Ran away, that he did, quick as lightning,　　Ratto, ratto il birbone è fuggito,
Got away, but I can't tell you where.　　E ad un tratto di vista m'usci.

SUSANNA
(*sottovoce to Figaro*)

Cherubino ...　　　　　　　　　　Sai che il paggio ...

FIGARO
(*sottovoce to Susanna*)

I know, for I saw him.　　　　　　So tutto, lo vidi.
(*laughing aloud*)
Ha, ha, ha, ha!　　　　　　　　　Ah, ah, ah, ah!

COUNT
(*to Figaro*)

Stop that noise! Now at once, hush I say!　　Taci là! taci là!

ANTONIO

　　　　What's the joke, pray?　　　　　　　　Cosa ridi?
Say, what is there here to laugh at?　　Cosa ridi? cosa ridi?

FIGARO
(*to Antonio*)

Why, how can we believe what you say,　　Tu sei cotto dal sorger del di,
When you're drunk at this hour of the day?　　Tu sei cotto dal sorger del di!

COUNT
(to Antonio)

Let me hear the story clearly now; a man from that window ...

Or ripetimi, ripetimi: un uom dal balcone ...

ANTONIO

From that window ...

Dal balcone ...

COUNT

Into the garden ...

In giardino ...

ANTONIO

Into the garden ...

In giardino.

SUSANNA, COUNTESS, AND FIGARO

Take no notice, my lord, he's been drinking!

Ma, signore, se in lui parla il vino!

COUNT
(to Antonio)

Yes, continue. Did you see his face, then?

Segui pure. Nè in volto vedesti?

ANTONIO

That I did not.

No, nol vidi.

SUSANNA AND COUNTESS
(sottovoce to Figaro)

You hear! Figaro, listen!

Olà, Figaro, ascolta.

FIGARO
(to Antonio)

Oh, you maudlin old fool, do be quiet!

Via, piangione, sta' zitto una volta:

(touching the flowers contemptuously)

What a fuss for a couple of flowers. If you want them to know who the man was

Per tre soldi far tanto tumulto! Giacchè il fatto non può stare occulto:

Who jumped down from the window, 'twas I.

Sono io stesso saltato di lì.

COUNT

Oh! 'Twas you then?

Chi? voi stesso?

COUNTESS AND SUSANNA
(aside)

I knew he would save us!

Che testa! che ingegno!

FIGARO
(to the Count)

Yes, of course.

Che stupor?

COUNT

I cannot believe it.

Già creder nol posso.

ANTONIO
(to Figaro)

Well, you've grown a good deal since your fall, then, I would swear you were just half the size.

Come mai diventaste si grosso? Dopo il salto non foste cosi.

FIGARO

That's because you'd the sun in your eyes.

A chi salta succede cosi.

ANTONIO

Who'd have thought it?

Chi'l direbbe?

Does he still contradict you?   Ed insiste, quel pazzo!

COUNT

What do you say?   Tu che dici?

ANTONIO

'Twas that boy, I'll be sworn, Sir.   A me parve il ragazzo.

COUNT
(excitedly)

Cherubin?   Cherubin!

SUSANNA AND COUNTESS
(aside)

Now we're ruined!   Maledetto!

FIGARO
(sarcastically)

Why of course, Sir.   Esso appunto.
Then he must have returned here on   Da Siviglia a cavallo qui giunto,
horseback,
For today he went off to the town.   Da Siviglia oggi forse sarà.

ANTONIO
(slow and stupid)

No, I'm sure that he was not on horseback,   Questo no, questo no: chè il cavallo
For no horse from the window came down.   Io non vidi saltare di là.

COUNT

Give me patience! No more of this   Che pazienza! Finiam questo ballo!
nonsense!

COUNTESS AND SUSANNA
(aside)

We are lost, no escape can I find.   Come mai, giusto ciel, finirà?

COUNT
(to Figaro, excitedly)

So 'twas you?   Dunque, tu ...

FIGARO
(cooly)

Yes, 'twas I.   Saltai giù.

COUNT

Then say why.   Ma perchè?

FIGARO

Fear of you.   Il timor ...

COUNT

Fear of me?   Che timor?

FIGARO
(pointing to the servants' quarters)

'Twas like this, Sir,   Là rinchiuso,
I was waiting in there for Susanna,   Aspettando quel caro visetto ...
When I heard such a babel of voices.   Tippe tappe, un susurro fuor d'uso ...
Yours was angry; I thought of this letter ...   Voi gridaste ... lo scritto biglietto ...
So I jumped from this window in terror, Saltai giù dal terrore confuso ...
(rubbing his foot as if he had hurt himself)
And I twisted my foot in the fall.   E stravolto m'ho un nervo del piè!

[28]

ANTONIO

I suppose that this paper which I picked up
Is yours then ...

Vostre, dunque, saran queste carte
Che perdeste ...

(He holds some folded papers out to Figaro: the Count takes them from him.)

COUNT

Oho! I'll have it now!

Olà, porgile a me.

FIGARO
(sottovoce to Susanna and the Countess)

Now he's done for me.

Sono in trappola.

SUSANNA AND COUNTESS
(sottovoce to Figaro)

Sharpen your wits, man.

Figaro, all'erta!

COUNT
(He opens the document, then immediately folds it up again.)

Tell me now what this paper can be.

Dite un po', questo foglio cos'è?

FIGARO

Wait one moment ... that paper ... I've so
many.

Tosto ... tosto ... n'ho tanti, aspettate.

(He pulls various papers out of his pockets and pretends to look at them.)

ANTONIO

I should think it's a list of your creditors.

Sarà forse il sommario de' debiti.

FIGARO

No, the wineshops, more likely.

No, la lista degli osti.

COUNT
(to Figaro)

Come, tell me.

Parlate.

(to Antonio)

You can leave us now.

E tu lascialo!

COUNTESS, SUSANNA AND FIGARO
(to Antonio)

Leave us now, and quickly.

Lascia $\begin{cases} \text{lo!} \\ \text{mi!} \end{cases}$ E parti!

ANTONIO

Just you wait till I catch you again, Sir!

Parto, sì, ma se torno a trovarti ...

(Exit.)

FIGARO

You can do what you like, I don't care.

Vanne, vanne, non temo di te.

COUNT
(He opens the paper once more and folds it up again. To Figaro.)

Well, Sir?

Dunque?

COUNTESS
(to Susanna, sottovoce)

Oh, heaven, 'tis the page's commission!

O ciel! la patente del paggio!

SUSANNA
(sottovoce to Figaro)

'Tis the page's commission ...

Giusti Dei! la patente! ...

COUNT
(to Figaro, ironically)

I'm waiting.

Coraggio!

FIGARO
(as if suddenly remembering)

Oh, my memory! Of course, the commission
Which the boy left a few hours ago.

Uh, che testa! Quest'è la patente
Che poc'anzi il fanciullo mi diè.

What was that for? Per che fare?

It needed ... Vi manca ...

It needed ... Vi manca?

Needed sealing ... Il suggello ...

Needed sealing. Il suggello!

Come, tell me. Rispondi?

Well, it's usual ... È l'usanza ...

Come, answer me quick, Sir! Su via: ti confondi?

Well, it's usual to seal a commission. È l'usanza di porvi il suggello.

Oh, the rascal's too much for my patience. Questo birbo mi toglie il cervello.
There is something concealed from me Tutto, tutto è un mistero per me.
here.

(*throwing down the paper in a passion*)

If we weather the storm now in safety, Se mi salvo da questa tempesta,
We shall not have a shipwreck to fear. Più non havvi naufragio per me.

You may bluster and rage as you like, Sir, Sbuffa invano, e la terra calpesta;
But I know more than you do, it's clear. Poverino, ne sa men di me.

Scene Twelve. *The Count, Countess, Susanna, Figaro, Marcellina, Bartolo and Basilio.*

We appear before your lordship Voi, signor, che giusto siete,
To demand a lawful right. Ci dovete or ascoltar.

Here's the moment for which I've Son venuti a vendicarmi,
waited,
And my revenge is at last in sight. Io mi sento consolar.

Here's another complication; Son venuti a sconcertarmi,
Worse than ever is our plight. Qual rimedio ritrovar?

FIGARO
(to the Count)

What's the cause of this intrusion?	Son tre stolidi, tre pazzi,
Mad they surely are, all three!	Cosa mai vengono a far?

COUNT

I forbid these interruptions;	Pian pianin, senza schiamazzi
Let them state their case to me.	Dica ognun quel che gli par.

MARCELLINA

This man here has signed a contract,	Un impegno nuziale
Signed a contract to espouse me,	Ha costui con me contratto;
And I make an application	E pretendo che il contratto
That the contract be fulfilled.	Deva meco effettuar.

COUNTESS, FIGARO AND SUSANNA

What's this? A contract?	Come! come!

COUNT

I must have silence!	Olà, silenzio:
'Tis for me to judge this case.	Io son qui per giudicar.

BARTOLO

I appear, Sir, for this lady,	Io da lei scelto avvocato,
As her counsel in this action,	Vengo a far le sue difese,
For performance of the contract,	Le legittime pretese
And for damages in full.	Io vi vengo a palesar.

COUNTESS, FIGARO AND SUSANNA

Purely spiteful in this action!	È un birbante!

COUNT

Once more I tell you, be silent;	Olà, silenzio!
'Tis for me to judge this case.	Io son qui per giudicar.

BASILIO

I bear witness that the plaintiff	Io, com'uom al mondo cognito,
Lent him money on condition	Vengo qui per testimonio
That if he could not repay her	Del promesso matrimonio
He to marry her agreed.	Con prestanza di danar.

COUNTESS, FIGARO AND SUSANNA

Do not listen to this talking;	Son tre matti! son tre matti!
All the three of them are crazy!	Son tre matti! son tre matti!

COUNT

The contract shall now be read over,	Lo vedremo:
And the truth I myself will soon discover.	Il contratto leggeremo.
All in order shall proceed.	Tutto in ordin deve andar.

COUNT, MARCELLINA, BARTOLO AND BASILIO
(aside)

All turns out as we expected:	Che bel colpo, che bel caso:
We'll soon make him look dejected;	È cresciuto a tutti il naso!
It was really providential	Qualche Nume a noi propizio
That $\begin{Bmatrix} they \\ we \end{Bmatrix}$ all came here just now.	Qui $\begin{Bmatrix} li \\ ci \end{Bmatrix}$ ha fatti capitar.

COUNTESS, FIGARO AND SUSANNA[*]

Here's confusion worse confounded!	Son confus $\begin{Bmatrix} a, \\ o, \end{Bmatrix}$ son stordit $\begin{Bmatrix} a, \\ o, \end{Bmatrix}$
By misfortunes we're surrounded;	Disperat $\begin{Bmatrix} a, \\ o, \end{Bmatrix}$ sbalordit $\begin{Bmatrix} a! \\ o! \end{Bmatrix}$
'Twas the devil, I am certain	Certo, un diavol dell'inferno
Sent these people here just now.	Qui li ha fatti capitar.

---

[*] In this passage the two soprano lines are often exchanged. See page 45.

Act Three

Scene One. *A state room with two thrones, prepared for the wedding feast. The Count alone. / Recitative*

COUNT
(aside, walking up and down)

What a strange situation! An anonymous letter,	Che imbarazzo è mai questo! Un foglio anonimo . . .
And then the maid locked up inside the dressing-room,	La cameriera in gabinetto chiusa . . .
With my lady so embarrassed – a man who jumps	La padrona confusa . . . un uom che salta
Into the garden from the window, and then the other	Dal balcone in giardino . . . un altro, appresso,
Who says that he did . . .	Che dice esser quel desso . . .
What on earth can it mean? Could it have been	Non so cosa pensar: potrebbe forse
Some young man of my dependants? There is no limit	Qualcun de' miei vassalli . . . a simil razza
To what they will dare. But then the Countess –	È comune l'ardir . . . Ma la Contessa . . .
No, I will not insult her; she has too high	Ah, che un dubbio l'offende . . . ella rispetta
A sense of her dignity, of my honour.	Troppo se stessa; e l'onor mio . . . l'onore . . .
Human nature is frail, I must admit it!	Dove diamin l'ha posto umano errore!

Scene Two. *The Count, Countess and Susanna.*

Enter the Countess and Susanna, unnoticed by the Count. They stop at the rear of the stage.

COUNTESS

There, don't be frightened; tell him	Via, fatti core: digli
To meet you in the garden.	Che ti attenda in giardino.

COUNT
(aside)

I wonder if Cherubino	Saprò se Cherubino
Ever went to Seville? The answer	Era giunto a Siviglia: a tale oggetto
Will soon come from Basilio.	Ho mandato Basilio . . .

SUSANNA

But Madam, if Figaro –	Oh, cielo! e Figaro . . .

COUNTESS

Don't say a word to Figaro! This assignation	A lui non dei dir nulla: in vece tua
Shall be kept by myself.	Voglio andarci io medesma.

COUNT
(as before)

Before this evening Basilio should be back.	Dovrebbe ritornar . . . Avanti sera

SUSANNA

My lady, I dare not.	Oddio! Non oso.

COUNTESS

Remember, all my happiness depends on it.	Pensa ch'è in tua man il mio riposo.

(She hides.)

COUNT
(as before)

And Susanna? who knows? she may have told her ladyship	E Susanna? Chi sa ch'ella tradito

All I said to her; oh, if she has done,   Abbia il segreto mio . . . Oh, se ha parlato,
Figaro shall marry the old harridan.   Gli fo sposar la vecchia.

SUSANNA
(aside)

Marcellina!   Marcellina!
(to the Count)

     My lord!   Signor . . .

COUNT
(in earnest)

     And what do you want?   Cosa bramate?

SUSANNA

My lord, have I offended you?   Mi par che siate in collera!

COUNT

Come tell me, what's your business?   Volete qualche cosa?

SUSANNA

My lord, my lady sent me –   Signor . . . la vostra sposa
She has her usual vapours,   Ha i soliti vapori,
And desires you would lend her your   E vi chiede il fiaschetto degli odori.
    smelling bottle.

COUNT

Pray take it.   Prendete.

SUSANNA

     I'll bring it back soon.   Or vel riporto.

COUNT

         No, no, pray keep it,   Ah, no: potete
You may want it yourself.   Ritenerlo per voi.

SUSANNA

        Myself?   Per me?
Girls in my position   Questi non son mali
Don't have ailments of that sort.   Da donne triviali.

COUNT

Not even a girl who lost her bridegroom   Un'amante che perde il caro sposo
An hour before the wedding?   Sul punto d'ottenerlo . . .

SUSANNA

We'll pay off Marcellina   Pagando Marcellina
With the dowry that you so kindly   Con la dote che voi mi prometteste . . .
    promised.

COUNT

You say I promised? When pray?   Ch'io vi promisi? Quando?

SUSANNA

I thought I understood so.   Credea d'averlo inteso . . .

COUNT

Yes, if you'd been inclined   Si, se voluto aveste
To come to an understanding.   Intendermi voi stessa.

SUSANNA

     If that is all, Sir,   È mio dovere;
I hope I know my duty towards your   E quel di sua Eccellenza è il mio volere.
    lordship.

No. 16. Duet

COUNT

Oh, why are you so cruel,   [30]   Crudel! Perchè finora
Why must I ask in vain?   Farmi languir così?

SUSANNA

My lord, a woman's answer   Signor, la donna ognora
Must not be made too plain.   Tempo ha di dir di sì.

COUNT

Then you'll be there this evening?   Dunque, in giardin verrai?

SUSANNA

As you desire, I will.   Se piace a voi, verrò.

COUNT

Promise you will not fail me.   E non mi mancherai?

SUSANNA

My word I shall fulfil.   No, non vi mancherò.

COUNT
(*aside*)

Oh, joy past all expressing,   [31]   Mi sento dal contento
All my desire to obtain.   Pieno di gioia il cor.

SUSANNA
(*aside*)

Forgive me all ye lovers   Scusatemi se mento,
That I deceive and feign.   Voi che intendete amor.

Recitative

COUNT

Tell me, why were you so   E perchè fosti meco
Distant with me this morning?   Stamattina sì austera?

SUSANNA

With Cherubino listening?   Col paggio ch'ivi c'era . . .

COUNT

      And with Basilio,   Ed a Basilio,
Who spoke on my behalf?   Che per me ti parlò . . .

SUSANNA

     What need have we   Ma qual bisogno
Of a man like Basilio?   Abbiam noi che un Basilio . . .

COUNT

    You're right there, I grant you.   È vero, è vero.
Promise again, Susanna,   E mi prometti, poi . . .
You will not disappoint me? The smelling- Se tu manchi, o cor mio . . . Ma la
  bottle!   Contessa
My lady will be waiting!   Attenderà il fiaschetto.

SUSANNA

     Oh, that was nothing;   Eh, fu un pretesto:
I had to make up some excuse for speaking. Parlato io non avrei, senza di questo.

COUNT
(*He takes her hand; she retreats.*)

You angel.   Carissima!

SUSANNA

    There's someone!   Vien gente.

COUNT
(*aside*)

    Now I am sure of her.   È mia senz'altro.

SUSANNA
(*aside*)

Oh, take your lips away, you scheming Forbitevi la bocca, o signor scaltro.
  rascal.

(*She tries to leave and meets Figaro in the doorway.*)

95

Scene Three. *The Count, Susanna and Figaro.*

FIGARO

Oh, Susanna! You here?	Ehi, Susanna, ove vai?

SUSANNA

Quiet, no need for a lawyer;	Taci. Senza avvocato
We are sure of our case now.	Hai già vinta la causa.

(*Exit.*)

FIGARO

What has happened?	Cosa è nato?

(*He follows her.*)

*Scene Four. *The Count alone. / No. 17. Recitative and Aria*

COUNT

We are sure of our case now! Yes, she said so!	Hai già vinto la causa! Cosa sento!
There's a trap to deceive me! Treachery! How dare they?	In qual laccio cadea! Perfidi! Io voglio
I'll punish them without any mercy; when I pass sentence,	Di tal modo punirvi . . . A piacer mio
They shall know who I am. But then supposing	La sentenza sarà . . . Ma s'ei pagasse
He paid off Marcellina?	La vecchia pretendente?
He, pay her? How could he do it? Besides Antonio	Pagarla! In qual maniera? . . . E poi v'è Antonio
Would refuse to let Susanna marry Figaro,	Che a un incognito Figaro ricusa
A foundling who knows nothing of his parents.	Di dare un nipote in matrimonio
I shall flatter the old idiot –	Coltivando l'orgoglio
He's as proud as a peacock –	Di questo mentecatto . . .
This is all in my favour; I'll wait no longer.	Tutto giova a un raggiro . . . Il colpo è fatto!

Aria

Must I forego my pleasure,	[32]	Vedrò, mentr'io sospiro,
While serf of mine rejoices?		Felice un servo mio?
Must I renounce my passion,		E un ben che invan desio
He have his heart's desire?		Ei posseder dovrà?
Must I behold my charmer		Vedrò per man d'amore
To low-born clown united?		Unita a un vile oggetto
While I for her am burning,		Chi in me destò un affetto
Dare she disdain my fire?		Che per me poi non ha?
No! I'll show you I'm your master,		Ah, no! Lasciarti in pace
No more will you defy me;		Non vo' questo contento!
Dare you be so presumptuous,		Tu non nascesti, audace!
As venture thus to thwart me?		Per dare a me tormento,
Dare you, my servant, laugh at me		E forse ancor per ridere
While I am mortified?		Di mia infelicità.
I will endure no longer,	[33]	Già la speranza sola
Vengeance alone inspires me,		Delle vendette mie
'Tis vengeance, only vengeance		Quest'anima consola
Can satisfy my pride.		E giubilar mi fa.

(*As he is leaving he meets Don Curzio.*)

Scene Five. *The Count, Marcellina, Figaro, Bartolo and Don Curzio; then Susanna. / Recitative.*

DON CURZIO
(*entering followed by Marcellina, Bartolo and Figaro*)

The case is decided:	È decisa la lite:
He must marry her or pay her. That's what the court says.	"O pagarla, o sposarla". Ora ammutite.

---

* See page 47 for a note on the order of scenes in Act Three.

MARCELLINA

Now I'm happy.   Io respiro.

FIGARO

And I'm wretched!   Ed io moro.

MARCELLINA
(aside)

At last the man I love will have to marry   Alfin sposa io sarò d'un uom che adoro.
me.

FIGARO
(to the Count)

I lodge an appeal, my lord.   Eccellenza, m'appello ...

COUNT

The judgment is a just one: È giusta la sentenza:
You will marry or pay. Bravo, Don   "O pagar, o sposar". Bravo Don Curzio.
Curzio.

DON CURZIO

Your lordship's humble servant!   Bontà di sua Eccellenza.

BARTOLO

'Tis a very sound judgment.   Che superba sentenza!

FIGARO

You think it sound, Sir?   In che, superba?

BARTOLO

Yes, for we're all avenged now.   Siam tutti vendicati.

FIGARO

I'll never marry her.   Io non la sposerò.

BARTOLO

Oh, yes, you will, Sir.   La sposerai.

DON CURZIO

You must marry her or pay her; did she   "O pagarla, o sposarla". Lei t'ha prestati
not lend you
Two thousand silver crowns, Sir?   Duemila pezzi duri.

FIGARO

I am a nobleman, and I cannot   Son gentiluomo, e senza
Marry without the consent of my parents.   L'assenso de' miei nobili parenti ...

COUNT

Of your parents? Who are they?   Dove sono? chi sono?

FIGARO

I wish someone would find them;   Lasciate ancor cercarli:
For the last ten years I've been looking for   Dopo dieci anni io spero di trovarli.
them everywhere.

BARTOLO

So you were found on the doorstep?   Qualche bambin trovato? ...

FIGARO

No, but lost there, I think, or rather stolen.   No, perduto, dottor; anzi rubato.

COUNT

Stolen?   Come?

MARCELLINA

Stolen?   Cosa?

BARTOLO

Your proof, Sir!   La prova?

DON CURZIO

Documentary?   Il testimonio?

FIGARO

Proofs? Yes, indeed, Sir! The fine   L'oro, le gemme e i ricamati panni,
  embroidered clothing,
Yes, and the jewels and gold too   Che ne' più teneri anni
Found on me by the robbers when they   Mi ritrovaro addosso i masnadieri,
  stole me, –
What better proof is wanted   Sono gl'indizi veri
Of my birth and my breeding? And, in   Di mia nascita illustre; e sopra tutto
  addition,
Here on my arm a very curious   Questo al mio braccio impresso geroglifico.
  birthmark –

MARCELLINA

What? A strawberry mark upon your right   Una spatola impressa al braccio destro? . . .
  arm?

FIGARO

And how did you know?   E a voi ch'il disse?

MARCELLINA

      Oh, heavens!   Oddio!
'Tis he then . . .   È desso . . .

FIGARO

    'Tis I indeed, ma'am.   È ver, son io.

DON CURZIO

Who?   Chi?

COUNT

Who?   Chi?

BARTOLO

Who?   Chi?

MARCELLINA

    Little Raphael.   Raffaello.

BARTOLO

By robbers you were stolen?   E i ladri ti rapir? . . .

FIGARO

    Yes, near a castle.   Presso un castello.

BARTOLO

Behold your mother.   Ecco tua madre.

FIGARO

    My nurse-maid?   Balia . . .

BARTOLO

    No, your mother.   No, tua madre.

COUNT AND DON CURZIO

His mother!   Sua madre?

FIGARO

    What can this mean?   Cosa sento!

MARCELLINA

    There stands your father!   Ecco tuo padre.

(She runs up to Figaro and embraces him.)

98

No. 18. Sextet

Oh, my long-lost child, embrace me, [34]
Let your mother's arms enfold you!

Riconosci in questo amplesso
Una madre, amato figlio.

FIGARO
(to Bartolo)

Father dear, now I have found you,
Don't refuse to do the same.

Padre mio, fate lo stesso:
Non mi fate più arrossir.

BARTOLO
(embracing Figaro)

Conscience tells me I'm your father,
And you now shall bear my name.

Resistenza la coscienza
Far non lascia al tuo desir.

DON CURZIO
(aside)

He's his father? And she's his mother?
Then the contract must be void.

Ei suo padre, ella sua madre:
L'imeneo non può seguir.

COUNT
(aside)

I'm astounded, I'm confounded;
All my hopes are now destroyed.

Son smarrito, son stordito:
Meglio è assai di qua partir.

MARCELLINA

I'm your mother!

Figlio amato!

BARTOLO

I'm your father!

Figlio amato!

FIGARO

My long-lost father!
My long-lost mother!

Parenti amati!
Parenti amati!

(The Count is about to leave, but Susanna stops him as she enters with a purse in her hand.)

SUSANNA

Please your lordship, wait a moment.
Here, I have the money ready,
I will pay the fine for Figaro,
And then you will set him free.

Alto, alto, signor Conte:
Mille doppie son qui pronte.
A pagar vengo per Figaro,
Ed a porlo in libertà.

COUNT AND DON CURZIO

'Tis too late, the case is settled;
Just look there and you will see.

Non sappiam com'è la cosa:
Osservate un poco là.

(Susanna turns round and sees Figaro embracing Marcellina. She makes as if to leave.)

SUSANNA

He's embracing Marcellina!
Is it true he's false to me?

Già d'accordo colla sposa:
Giusti Dei, che infedeltà!

(to Figaro)

False and faithless!

Lascia, iniquo!

FIGARO
(He holds her back; she struggles.)

Stay a moment!
Hear me, my dearest.

No, t'arresta.
Senti, o cara.

SUSANNA
(slapping him)

Here's my answer.

Senti questa.

FIGARO, BARTOLO AND MARCELLINA

Here's resounding proof of passion,
All for love she struck the blow.

È un effetto di buon core:
Tutto amore è quel che fa.

COUNT AND DON CURZIO

All{my/our} plans are in confusion, Frem{o,/e,} smani{o/a} dal furore;

Fate decrees{my/our} overthrow. Il destino{me la/gliela} fa.

SUSANNA

Must I see myself deserted? Fremo, smanio dal furore,
Why, she's twice his age, I know. Una vecchia me la fa.

MARCELLINA
(*to Susanna*)

Be calm and embrace me, Lo sdegno calmate,
My dearest Susanna, Mia cara figliuola,
For I am his mother Sua madre abbracciate,
And yours shall be too. Che or vostra sarà.

(*She runs up to Susanna and embraces her.*)

SUSANNA

His mother? [35] Sua madre?

ALL

His mother! Sua madre.

FIGARO

And this is my father; E quello è mio padre,
He swears it is true. Che a te lo dirà.

SUSANNA

His father? Suo padre?

ALL

His father! Suo padre.

FIGARO

And this is my mother, E quella è mia madre,
Who swears it is true. Che a te lo dirà.

(*All four run to embrace one another.*)

SUSANNA, FIGARO, MARCELLINA AND BARTOLO

Oh, moment of rapture, Al dolce contento
What joys are before us! Di questo momento,
Our troubles are over, Quest'anima appena
Our cares are at rest. Resistere or sa.

How happy the fortune Al dolce contento
That brings us together, Di questo momento,
United at last Quest'anima appena
To all those we love best. Resistere or sa.

COUNT AND DON CURZIO

They soon shall repent it, Al fiero tormento
Their joy shall be fleeting, Di questo momento,
Although for the moment Quest'anima appena
Our failure's confessed. Resistere or sa.

We will not be thwarted, Al fiero tormento
We'll still have our vengeance, Di questo momento,
Who dares to oppose us Quest'anima appena
Shall find it no jest. Resistere or sa.

(*Exeunt the Count and Don Curzio.*)

Scene Six. *Susanna, Marcellina, Figaro and Bartolo. / Recitative*

MARCELLINA
(*to Bartolo*)

To think that we have found him, the little darling
That we used to be so fond of . . .

Eccovi, o caro amico, il dolce frutto
Dell'antico amor nostro . . .

BARTOLO

I thought that little episode
Was buried in oblivion. Well, as we've found him
I'll admit that he's my son.
I suppose that I shall have to marry you now.

Or non parliamo
Di fatti sì remoti. Egli è mio figlio:
Mia consorte voi siete;
E le nozze farem quando volete.

MARCELLINA

Today! We'll have a double wedding.
(*to Figaro, giving him the contract*)
Take this; here is the contract
For the money you owe me, as a wedding present.

Oggi, e doppie saranno.

Prendi, questo è il biglietto
Del danar che a me devi; ed è tua dote.

SUSANNA
(*throwing down the purse of money*)

Take this from milady.

Prendi ancor questa borsa.

BARTOLO
(*doing the same*)

And this from me too!

E questa ancora.

FIGARO

Thank you! I'll take as much as you like to give me.

Bravi: gettate pur, ch'io piglio ognora.

SUSANNA

Now we must go and tell all our good fortune
To my lady and my uncle.
Could anyone be happier in all the world than I am?

Voliamo ad informar d'ogni avventura
Madama e nostro zio.
Chi al par di me contento?

FIGARO

I am!

Io.

BARTOLO

I am!

Io.

MARCELLINA

I am!

Io.

SUSANNA, FIGARO, MARCELLINA AND BARTOLO

And if my lord is furious, so much the better!

E schiatti il signor Conte al gusto mio!

(*Exeunt embracing one another.*)

Scene Seven. *Barbarina and Cherubino.*

BARBARINA

Come on, come on, Cherubino; we'll go to my house.
Who do you think you'll find there?
All the prettiest girls there are in the village;
But you'll be prettier far than any of them.

Andiam, andiam, bel paggio: in casa mia
Tutte ritroverai
Le più belle ragazze del castello.
Di tutte sarai tu certo più bello.

CHERUBINO

Oh, Barbarina, if his lordship

Ah! Se il Conte mi trova,

101

Should find me there? You know	Misero me! Tu sai
That he thinks I have ridden off to Seville.	Che partito ei mi crede per Siviglia.

BARBARINA

Oh, does he really think so? Well if he finds you,	Oh, ve' che maraviglia! E se ti trova,
It won't be the first time.	Non sarà cosa nuova.
Listen, we're going to dress you up like one of us now,	Odi, vogliam vestirti come noi:
Then we'll all go together,	Tutte insieme andrem poi
To take a bunch of flowers to my lady.	A presentar de' fiori a Madamina.
I shall take care of you, dear Cherubino.	Fidati, o Cherubin, di Barbarina.

(*Exeunt.*)*

Scene Eight. *The Countess alone. / No. 19. Recitative and Aria*

COUNTESS

Is Susanna not here? I'm impatient	E Susanna non vien! Son ansiosa
To be told what his lordship	Di saper come il Conte
Has said to her proposal. And yet I'm doubtful	Accolse la proposta. Alquanto ardito
If it was not too bold; my lord is always	Il progetto mi par; ad uno sposo
So impulsive and jealous.	Sì vivace e geloso...
But what's the harm? I keep the assignation	Ma che mal c'è? Cangiando i miei vestiti
Disguised as Susanna, while she wears my dress ...	Con quelli di Susanna, e i suoi co' miei ...
Under cover of darkness. Oh, heavens, what a	Al favor della notte ... O cielo! A quale
Humiliation I suffer! Oh, cruel husband,	Umil stato fatale io son ridotta
To reduce me to this! Did ever woman	Da un consorte crudel; che, dopo avermi,
Have to bear such a life	Con un misto inaudito
Of neglect and desertion, such jealous fury, such insults?	D'infedeltà, di gelosie, di sdegno,
Once he loved me, then disdained me, and now betrays me;	Prima amata, indi offesa, e alfin tradita,
Ah! Must I now beg for a servant's favour?	Fammi or cercar da una mia serva aita!

Aria

I remember days long departed,	[36]	Dove sono i bei momenti
Days when love no end could know;		Di dolcezza e di piacer,
I remember fond vows and fervent –		Dove andaro i giuramenti
All were broken long ago.		Di quel labbro menzogner?
Oh, then, why, if I was fated		Perchè mai, se in pianti e in pene
From that height of joy to fall,		Per me tutto si cangiò,
Must I still those happy moments		La memoria di quel bene
In my hour of pain recall?		Dal mio sen non trapassò?
Dare I hope to be rewarded?		Ah! se almen la mia costanza
Must I languish all in vain?		Nel languire amando ognor
Some day, surely, my devotion		Mi portasse una speranza
Might his faithless heart regain.		Di cangiar l'ingrato cor.

(*Exit.*)

Scene Nine. *The Count and Antonio. / Recitative*

ANTONIO
(*with a hat in his hand*)

I swear to you, my lord, that Cherubino	Io vi dico, signor, che Cherubino
Is still hanging around here;	È ancora nel castello:
And here's his hat to prove it.	E vedete per prova il suo cappello.

COUNT

But how can he be here still?	Ma come, se a quest'ora
If he ought by this time to be at Seville?	Esser giunto a Siviglia egli dovria?

---

* The arietta *'Se così brami'* for Cherubino was included at this point in the first printed libretto, and there are references to it in the autograph score, but no music has survived for it.

ANTONIO

Excuse me, Sir, but today Seville's at my house.	Scusate, oggi Siviglia è a casa mia.
There they've dressed him as a girl, Sir, And there he's left all his other clothes behind.	Là vestissi da donna, e là lasciati Ha gli altri abiti suoi.

COUNT

The devil he has!	Perfidi!

ANTONIO

Come with me and you'll see for yourself, Sir.	Andiam, e li vedrete voi.

(*Exeunt.*)

Scene Ten. *The Countess and Susanna.*

COUNTESS

What are you saying? And what did the Count say to that news?	Cosa mi narri! E che ne disse, il Conte?

SUSANNA

Oh, there was no mistaking That my lord's very angry.	Gli si leggeva in fronte Il dispetto e la rabbia.

COUNTESS

Wait though. It will be easier now to catch him. And where did you invite him To look for you this evening?	Piano: chè meglio or lo porremo in gabbia. Dov'è l'appuntamento Che tu gli proponesti?

SUSANNA

In the garden.	In giardino.

COUNTESS

We'll make it clearer. Write to hm.	Fissiamgli un loco. Scrivi.

SUSANNA

I write to him? Oh, my lady!	Ch'io scriva . . . Ma, signora . . .

COUNTESS

Write what I tell you, I take The whole responsibility.	Eh, scrivi, dico; e tutto Io prendo su me stessa.

(*Susanna sits down and writes.*)

Head it "Song to the breezes" . . .	Canzonetta sull' aria . . .

SUSANNA

The breezes . . .	Sull'aria . . .

No. 20. Duettino

COUNTESS
(*dictating*)

"How delightful 'tis to wander . . ."	[37] "Che soave zeffiretto . . ."

SUSANNA
(*repeating the words after the Countess*)

'Tis to wander . . .	Zeffiretto . . .

COUNTESS
(*as before*)

"By the breath of evening fanned . . ."	"Questa sera spirerà . . ."

SUSANNA
(*as before*)

By the breath of evening fanned . . .	Questa sera spirerà . . .

COUNTESS
(as before)

"Where the scented pines are closest."	"Sotto i pini del boschetto."

SUSANNA
(asking her)

Where the scented?	Sotto i pini?

(writing)

Where the scented pines are closest.	Sotto i pini del boschetto.

COUNTESS

And the rest he'll understand.	Ei già il resto capirà.

SUSANNA

Yes, the rest he'll understand.	Certo, certo: il capirà.

(They read the letter over again together.)

Recitative

SUSANNA

There is the letter, but what about a seal for it?	Piegato è il foglio ... Or come si sigilla?

COUNTESS
(handing her a pin)

I know: we'll put a pin through – That will do for a seal. One moment – just write On the back of the letter, "Send the seal back as answer".	Ecco, prendi una spilla: Servirà di sigillo. Attendi ... scrivi Sul riverso del foglio: "Rimandate il sigillo".

SUSANNA

He won't forget it, Like the seal of the commission!	È più bizzarro Di quel della patente.

COUNTESS

Put it away now; I hear some people coming.	Presto, nascondi ... Io sento venir gente.

(Susanna puts the note in her bosom.)

Scene Eleven. *The Countess, Susanna, Barbarina, Cherubino and peasant girls.*

Enter peasant girls carrying bouquets of flowers, led by Barbarina. Amongst them is Cherubino dressed like them. / No. 21. Chorus

CHORUS

Noble lady, here we offer Fairest flowers that we can find. They were plucked at early morning, Ere the sun on them had shined.	Ricevete, o padroncina, Queste rose e questi fior, Che abbiam colto stamattina Per mostrarvi il nostro amor.
Simple flowers are all we bring you, Simple songs are all we sing you, Of devotion, love, and duty, To our lady fair and kind.	Siamo tante contadine, E siam tutte poverine: Ma quel poco che rechiamo Ve lo diamo di buon cor.

Recitative

BARBARINA

If it pleases your ladyship, We are girls from the village; We hope that you will not refuse these flowers – They are all that we can give you, begging your pardon.	Queste sono, Madama, Le ragazze del loco, Che il poco ch'han vi vengono ad offrire, E vi chiedon perdon del loro ardire.

COUNTESS

I thank you for your kindness.	Oh, brave! Vi ringrazio.

SUSANNA

Aren't they charming, my lady?   Come sono vezzose!

COUNTESS
(*pointing out Cherubino*)

Tell me now, I'd like to know,   E chi è, narratemi,
Who is that pretty girl there?   Quell'amabil fanciulla
How very shy she's looking!   Ch'ha l'aria si modesta?

BARBARINA

That is one of my cousins; she came last   Ell'è una mia cugina, e per le nozze
night
To stay with us for the wedding.   È venuta ier sera.

COUNTESS

Then we ought to show honour to a   Onoriamo la bella forastiera.
stranger.
(*to Cherubino*)
Come here, my child, won't you give me   Venite qui . . . datemi i vostri fiori.
your flowers.
(*She takes Cherubino's flowers and kisses him on the forehead. Then aside*)
Look how she blushes!   Come arrossi!
(*to Susanna*)
Susanna, doesn't she remind you   Susanna, e non ti pare
Just a little bit of someone?   Che somigli ad alcuno?

SUSANNA

The very image!   Al naturale . . .

Scene Twelve. *The Countess, Susanna, Barbarina, Cherubino, the Count and Antonio.*
*Enter the Count and Antonio. The latter is carrying Cherubino's hat: he creeps quietly onto
the stage, takes the girl's cap off Cherubino's head and replaces it with the one he carries.*)

ANTONIO

Caught you at last, Sir! Here is the gallant   Eh, cospettaccio! È questi l'uffiziale.
captain!

COUNTESS
(*aside*)

Oh, heavens!   Oh, stelle!

SUSANNA
(*aside*)

Little rascal!   Malandrino!

COUNT
(*to the Countess*)

Well, my lady . . .   Ebben! Madama . . .

COUNTESS

I do assure your lordship,   Io sono, o signor mio,
I am just as surprised and irritated as you Irritata e sorpresa al par di voi.
are.

COUNT

But this morning?   Ma stamane?

COUNTESS

This morning   Stamane . . .
I admit we intended   Per l'odierna festa
To dress him up in girl's clothes, as you see Volevam travestirlo al modo stesso
him,
To make some fun this evening.   Che l'han vestito adesso.

COUNT
(*to Cherubino*)

What are you doing here?   E perchè non partiste?

105

CHERUBINO
(whipping his hat off his head)

My lord . . .   Signor . . .

COUNT

    You shall be punished   Saprò punire
For not obeying orders.   La sua disobbedienza.

BARBARINA

Please your lordship, please your lordship!   Eccellenza, Eccellenza,
You so often have said to me,   Voi mi dite si spesso,
When you came to see me, and hugged and   Qual volta m'abbracciate e mi baciate:
    kissed me,
"Barbarina, if you love me,   "Barbarina, se m'ami,
I'll give you all you ask for."   Ti darò quel che brami."

COUNT

Oh, did I say that?   Io, dissi questo?

BARBARINA

      Oh, yes.   Voi.
Now give me Cherubino   Or datemi, padrone,
To be my little husband,   In sposo Cherubino,
And I'll love you just like my little kitten.   E v'amerò com'amo il mio gattino.

COUNTESS
(to the Count)

My lord, I think it's your turn.   Ebbene: or tocca a voi . . .

ANTONIO
(to Barbarina)

      Good little girl!   Brava figliuola!
You're pretty sharp at picking up lessons.   Hai buon maestro che ti fa la scuola.

COUNT
(aside)

Is it a plot, of man, woman, or devil   Non so qual uom, qual demone, qual Dio
That puts me in the wrong at every   Rivolga tutto quanto a torto mio.
    moment?

Scene Thirteen. *The Countess, Susanna, Barbarina, Cherubino, peasant girls, the Count, Antonio and Figaro.*

FIGARO
(entering)

My lord, if you keep all these   Signor . . . se trattenete
Girls here waiting for nothing,   Tutte queste ragazze,
We shall not have any dancing.   Addio festa . . . addio danza . . .

COUNT

      Indeed? With your injured   E che! Vorresti
Foot you think of dancing?   Ballar col piè stravolto?

FIGARO
(He pretends to stretch his leg, then practices a few steps.)

I don't feel it much now.   Eh, non mi duol più molto.
(He calls the girls together, and is about to leave when the Count calls him back.)
Come, girls, the music's waiting!   Andiam, belle fanciulle . . .

COUNTESS
(sottovoce to Susanna)

How will he ever manage to escape now?   Come si caverà dall'imbarazzo?

SUSANNA
(sottovoce to the Countess)

Be sure he'll do it somehow.   Lasciate fare a lui.

Yes, it was lucky
You only damaged the flowerpots.

Per buona sorte
I vasi eran de creta.

FIGARO

You're quite right, Sir.
Now come along, girls, make haste there!

Senza fallo.
Andiamo, dunque, andiamo.

(*He tries to leave, but Antonio holds him back.*)

ANTONIO

And so Cherubino
Got on his horse and galloped off to
Seville.

E intanto, a cavallo,
Di galoppo a Siviglia andava il paggio.

FIGARO

Either galloped or trotted – well, good luck
to him!
(*on the point of leaving*)
Now girls, we must be leaving.

Di galoppo o di passo ... buon viaggio.

Venite, belle giovani.

COUNT
(*leading him back to the middle of the stage*)

And Cherubino left his
Commission in your pocket?

E a te la sua patente
Era in tasca rimasta ...

FIGARO

Yes, he did, Sir.
I can't think why you ask me.

Certamente.
Che razza di domanda!

ANTONIO
(*to Susanna who is making signals to Figaro*)

No good your making signals; he cannot
read them.
(*He takes Cherubino by the hand and presents him to Figaro.*)
Well, here is a young man
Who maintains my future nephew is a liar.

Via, non fargli più motti: ei non t'intende.

Ed ecco chi pretende
Che sia un bugiardo, il mio signor nipote.

FIGARO

Cherubino!

Cherubino!

ANTONIO

Yes, that's him.

Or ci sei.

FIGARO
(*to the Count*)

And what does he say?

Che diamin canta?

COUNT

That it was he who jumped down
Out of the window this morning onto the
flowerpots.

Non canta, no, ma dice
Ch'egli saltò stamane in sui garofani ...

FIGARO

Does he say so? Well then, if I could jump it,
He is lighter than I am,
Couldn't he do the same?

Ei lo dice! ... Sarà ... Se ho saltato io,
Si può dare che anch'esso
Abbia fatto lo stesso.

COUNT

You both jumped?

Anch'esso?

FIGARO

Why not?
I should not think of calling him a liar.

Perchè no?
Io non impugno mai quel che non so.

No. 22. Finale
(*A Spanish march is heard in the distance.*) [38]

Hark to the music, away now!

Ecco la marcia ... andiamo.

Come, take your places, you girls there,   A' vostri posti, o belle, a' vostri posti.
   take your places.
You take my arm Susanna.   Susanna, dammi il braccio.

SUSANNA

Here I am.   Eccolo.
(*Figaro takes Antonio with one arm and Susanna with the other, Exeunt all, except the Count and the Countess.*)

COUNT
(*aside*)

    This is shameless!   Temerari!

COUNTESS
(*aside*)

    Ah, how I tremble.   Io son di ghiaccio.
(*The march gets gradually louder.*)

COUNT

My lady!   Contessa . . .

COUNTESS

    Pray say no more, Sir.   Or non parliamo.
Here come the two happy couples,   Ecco qui le due nozze:
We must receive them now; besides,   Riceverle dobbiam; alfin si tratta
   there's one bride
Under your protection.   D'una vostra protetta.
Be seated.   Seggiamo.

COUNT

    I will, Ma'am,   Seggiamo.
(*aside*)
    And plan revenge upon them.   E meditiam vendetta.
(*They take their seats.*)

Scene Fourteen. *The Count, Countess, Figaro, Susanna, Bartolo, Marcellina, Cherubino, Barbarina, peasant women, labourers and huntsmen.*

Enter the huntsmen shouldering their guns; lawyers; peasant men and women; two young girls carrying the bridal cap adorned with white feathers; two more with the veil; two more with the gloves and a bouquet of flowers; two more young girls carrying another bridal cap for Susanna, and so on; Figaro with Marcellina; Bartolo with Susanna; Antonio, Barbarina and so on. Bartolo leads Susanna up to the Count and kneels before him to receive the cap, etc. from him. Figaro leads Marcellina up to the Countess and does the same.

TWO PEASANT WOMEN

Come all faithful lovers   Amanti costanti,
And join us in song,   Seguaci d'onor,
To him who released us   Cantate, lodate
From shame and from wrong.   Si saggio signor.

For never again will   Amanti costanti,
A bride from today   Seguaci d'onor,
The toll of her honour   Cantate, lodate
To him have to pay.   Si saggio signor.

Our virtue protecting   A un dritto cedendo
Our honour respecting,   Che oltraggia, che offende,
The right he renounces   Ei caste vi rende
Which brought us disgrace.   Ai vostri amator.

Then gratefully raising   A un dritto cedendo
Our voices we'll praise him,   Che oltraggia, che offende,
Who now gives us pure   Ei caste vi rende
To the bridegroom's embrace.   Ai vostri amator.

CHORUS

With grateful emotion   Cantiamo, lodiamo,

Our voices we raise,	Si saggio signor.
Our lord and our master	Cantiamo, lodiamo,
To honour and praise.	Si saggio signor.

(During the duet Susanna kneels. She plucks the Count's coat and shows him the note. Then she puts the hand nearest the audience to her head, whilst the Count, under pretence of adjusting her cap, takes the note from her. The Count puts it secretively in his breast. Susanna rises and curtseys; Figaro comes forward to receive her. They begin to dance the fandango. Marcellina rises a little after, and Bartolo comes forward to receive her from the hands of the Countess. The Count stands aside, takes out the note, and seems to prick his finger, shaking it, pressing it, and sucking it. Then he sees that the note is sealed with a pin, which he throws to the ground as he speaks. Meanwhile the orchestra is playing very softly.) [39]

COUNT

Ha, what's this pin to prick my finger?	Eh, già, si sa; solita usanza:
A pin to seal the letter! How like a woman!	Le donne ficcan gli aghi in ogni loco ...
Ha, ha! I see her meaning.	Ah! ah! Capisco il gioco.

FIGARO
(He sees the whole performance, and says to Susanna)

Look, his lordship is reading	Un biglietto amoroso
A loving little note from a lady.	Che gli diè nel passar qualche galante;
I think she must have sealed it with a pin.	Ed era sigillato d'una spilla
Look there, his lordship's pricked his finger.	Ond'egli si punse il dito.

(The Count reads the note, kisses it, hunts for the pin, finds it, and puts it in his silk cuff.)

| Now you see he has dropped the pin and cannot find it. | Il narciso or la cerca. Oh, che stordito! |

Recitative

COUNT

Good friends and neighbours, we'll celebrate this evening	Andate, amici! E sia per questa sera
The marriage of these two happy couples	Disposto l'apparato nuziale
In a right merry fashion. It is my wish	Colla più ricca pompa. Io vo' che sia
That the night should pass in feasting; we'll have dancing	Magnifica la festa; e canti e fochi,
And singing; after supper we'll have fireworks. I mean to show you	E gran cena e gran ballo. E ognuno impari
The reward that I give to faithful service.	Com'io tratto color che a me son cari.

CHORUS
(The Chorus and march are repeated, and all leave.)

CHORUS

Come all faithful lovers	Amanti costanti,
And join us in song,	Seguaci d'onor,
To him who released us	Cantate, lodate
From shame and from wrong.	Si saggio signor.

Our virtue protecting,	A un dritto cedendo
Our honour respecting,	Che oltraggia, che offende,
That right he renounces	Ei caste vi rende
Which brought us disgrace,	Ai vostri amator.
And pure gives the bride	Ei caste vi rende
To the bridegroom's embrace.	Ai vostri amator.

With grateful emotion	Cantiamo, lodiamo
Our voices we raise,	Si saggio signor.
Our lord and our master	Cantiamo, lodiamo
To honour and praise.	Si saggio signor.

Act Four

A closely-planted garden with two arbours, their entrances to right and left. Night.

Scene One. *Barbarina alone. / No. 23. Cavatina*

BARBARINA
(holding a paper lantern and searching for something on the ground)

I have lost it. Oh, how dreadful! Oh, [40]   L'ho perduta . . . me meschina! . . .
wherever can it be?
I have dropped it. Oh, how dreadful!   Ah, chi sa dove sarà?
Oh, what will they say to me?
No, 'tis useless, I cannot find it;   Non la trovo . . . E mia cugina . . .
Cousin Susanna and milord, what will   E il padron, cosa dirà?
they say?

Scene Two. *Barbarina, Figaro and Marcellina. / Recitative*

FIGARO
(entering with Marcellina)

What's the matter, Barbarina?   Barbarina, cos'hai?

BARBARINA

Oh, I've lost it, I've lost it!   L'ho perduta, cugino.

FIGARO

Lost what?   Cosa?

MARCELLINA

Lost what?   Cosa?

BARBARINA

          The pin   La spilla
That his lordship gave me   Che a me diede il padrone
To take back to Susanna.   Per recar a Susanna.

FIGARO

To Susanna! The pin!   A Susanna? la spilla?
      (angrily)
So already at your age   E così tenerella . . .
It seems you've begun to . . .   Il mestiere già sai . . .
      (quietly)
To go running on other people's errands? Di far tutto sì ben quel che tu fai?

BARBARINA

But why are you so angry now?   Cos'è vai meco in collera?

FIGARO

Can't you see I was joking? Look here, E non vedi ch'io scherzo? osserva . . .
child . . .

(He searches the ground for a moment, then adroitly removing a pin from Marcellina's coat or cap, he gives it to Barbarina.)

      Here is   Questa
The pin, the pin his lordship   È la spilla che il Conte
Gave you to take back to Susanna;   Da recare ti diede alla Susanna,
It was used, wasn't it, to seal a letter? E servia di sigillo a un bigliettino.
I know as much as you do.   Vedi s'io sono istrutto.

BABARINA

If you know as much as I, why do you ask E perchè il chiedi a me, quando sai tutto?
me?

110

FIGARO

I should like you to tell me how his lordship
Sent you on such an errand.

Avea gusto d'udir come il padrone
Ti diè la commissione.

BARBARINA

He just said to me,
"Here, Barbarina, take this pin and give it
To the lovely Susanna, and say to her,
'This is the seal of the pinewood'."

Che miracoli!
"Tieni, fanciulla, reca questa spilla
Alla bella Susanna, e dille: 'Questo
È il sigillo de' pini'."

FIGARO

Aha! The pinewood!

Ah, ah, de' pini!

BARBARINA

But I forgot, he told me,
"Don't let anyone see you".
But you'll not tell I told you?

È ver ch'ei mi soggiunse:
"Guarda che alcun non veda".
Ma tu, già, tacerai.

FIGARO

Oh, you can trust me.

Sicuramente.

BARBARINA

There's no harm if you know.

A te, già, niente preme.

FIGARO

If I know, of course not.

Oh, niente, niente.

BARBARINA

Goodbye, I must be going,
First to Susanna, and then to Cherubino.

Addio, mio bel cugino:
Vò da Susanna e poi da Cherubino.

(*She skips off.*)

Scene Three. *Figaro and Marcellina.*

FIGARO
(*dumbstruck*)

Mother!

Madre.

MARCELLINA

Dearest!

Figlio.

FIGARO

I'm ruined.

Son morto.

MARCELLINA

Try to regard it calmly.

Calmati, figlio mio.

FIGARO

My life is ruined.

Son morto, dico.

MARCELLINA

Patience, patience, always patience!
I know it's serious,
And requires careful thought. Now to begin with,
You do not know who's going to be the victim.

Flemma, flemma, e poi flemma:
il fatto è serio,
E pensarci convien. Ma guarda un poco
Che ancor non sai di chi si prenda gioco.

FIGARO

I do indeed, though. Why, mother, that is the pin
That he picked up in the ballroom.

Ah! quella spilla, o madre, è quella stessa
Che poc'anzi ei raccolse.

MARCELLINA

I know. But this is
No more than a warning

È ver ... Ma questo
Al più ti porge un dritto

111

| That you must watch them, and keep your eyes wide open. Still, you cannot be certain . . . | Di stare in guardia e vivere in sospetto: Ma non sai se in effetto . . . |

FIGARO

| But I will watch them! And thanks to Barbarina I shall know where to find them. | All'erta, dunque: il loco del congresso So dov'è stabilito. |

(He is about to leave.)

MARCELLINA

| Tell me where you are going. | Dove vai, figlio mio? |

FIGARO

| To avenge myself and the whole race of husbands. | A vendicar tutti i mariti. Addio. |

(He storms out.)

Scene Four. *Marcellina alone.*

MARCELLINA

| Quick, let me warn Susanna! I am sure she is innocent; she's so natural, So modest and so candid. And then, besides, Supposing she isn't . . . Well, now that I've no reason To be jealous any longer, Surely all women ought to support one another; When we think how we're treated By our husbands and lovers, oh, 'tis our duty. | Presto, avvertiam Susanna . . . Io la credo innocente: quella faccia . . . Quell'aria di modestia . . . È caso ancora Ch'ella non fosse . . . Ah! quando il cor non ci arma Personale interesse, Ogni donna è portata alla difesa Del suo povero sesso, Da questi uomini ingrati a torto oppresso. |

No. 24. Aria

Throughout the realm of nature, When springtime bids them pair, We see how every creature Its joy in peace can share.	Il capro e la capretta Son sempre in amistà; L'agnello all'agnelletta La guerra mai non fa;
The wildest and most cruel, Through pathless forest ranging Shows to his mate, unchanging, His love and tender care.	Le più feroci belve Per selve e per campagne Lascian le lor compagne In pace e libertà.
But we, poor hapless womankind, Who sacrifice our all to men, Receive from them but perfidy And pain that's hard to bear.	Sol noi, povere femmine, Che tanto amiam questi uomini, Trattate siam dai perfidi Ognor con crudeltà.

(Exit.)

Scene Five. *Barbarina alone. / Recitative*

BARBARINA
(carrying fruit and cakes)

| The arbour on the left hand, I think he told me; Is this it? Yes, that's right. I hope he won't forget me. These people are so hasty. I hardly got them to give me An orange or a biscuit. "And for whom is this supper?" "It's for a friend of mine, Sir". "I thought as much!" Well, well! His lordship hates him; but I shall always love him; | "Nel padiglione a manca", ei così disse. È questo, è questo . . . E poi, se non venisse? Ah, ah, che brava gente! A stento darmi Un arancio, una pera e una ciambella. "Per chi, madamigella?" "Oh, per qualcun, signore!" "Già lo sappiam." Ebbene: Il padron l'odia, ed io gli voglio bene! |

112

I had to pay a kiss for this – what does it matter?	Però costommi un bacio . . . E cosa importa?
Cherubino will pay it back.	Forse qualcun mel renderà . . .

(She hears someone coming.)

Oh, mercy!	Son morta!

Scene Six. *Figaro; then Bartolo, Basilio and workmen.*

FIGARO
(alone, with a cloak and lantern)

That's Barbarina.	È Barbarina . . .

(He hears people approaching.)

Who is this?	Chi va là?

BASILIO
(entering with Bartolo and a group of workmen)

You sent for us:	Son quelli
Here we are.	Che invitasti a venir.

BARTOLO

Why are you scowling	Che brutto ceffo!
Just like the villain in a play? What is the cause	Sembri un cospirator. Che diamin sono
Of this mysterious appointment?	Quegli infausti apparati?

FIGARO

You will see very shortly.	Lo vedrete tra poco.
You are invited here	In questo stesso loco
To witness the ancient privilege	Celebrerem la festa
Of the Lord of the Manor,	Della mia sposa onesta
Granted by my virtuous bride.	E del feudal signor . . .

BASILIO

Oh, shall we really?	Ah, buono, buono!
I see now how it stands.	Capisco come egli è.

(aside)

They've arranged this without employing me.	Accordati si son senza di me.

FIGARO

You will stay here and wait	Voi da questi contorni
Where no-one can see you. I have to	Non vi scostate. Intanto
Go and make further arrangements;	Io vado a dar certi ordini
I'll come back in a moment.	E torno in pochi istanti:
Then, when I whistle, you'll both rush out together.	A un fischio mio correte tutti quanti.

(Exeunt all except Bartolo and Basilio.)

Scene Seven. *Bartolo and Basilio.*

BASILIO

The man's possessed by devils!	Ha i diavoli nel corpo.

BARTOLO

What has upset him?	Ma cosa, quanti?

BASILIO

Nothing.	Nulla:
His lordship likes Susanna; she has given him	Susanna piace al Conte. Ella, d'accordo,
Tonight as an assignation,	Gli diè un appuntamento
Which Figaro does not like.	Ch'a Figaro non piace.

BARTOLO

But do you think he ought to suffer it in silence?	E che, dunque: dovria soffrirlo in pace?

Many a man has endured it;
Why should he make objections? And then, consider,
If he did, where's the gain? For in this world, friend,
To cross swords with the gentry
Is a dangerous pastime,
And in ninety per cent of cases, you'll be defeated.

Quel che soffrono tanti
Ei soffrir non potrebbe? E poi, sentite:

Che guadagno può far? Nel mondo, amico,

L'accozzarla co' grandi
Fu pericolo ognora:
Dàn novanta per cento, e han vinto ancora.

No. 25. Aria

Youth is headstrong, overbearing,
Too impulsive as a rule.
I myself was young and daring,
I was just as big a fool.

In quegli anni in cui val poco
La mal pratica ragion,
Ebbi anch'io lo stesso fuoco:
Fui quel pazzo ch'or non son.

But the passing years have brought me
Sense enough to swallow pride,
And experience at last has taught me
Not to swim against the tide.

Ma col tempo e coi perigli

Donna flemma capitò;
E i capricci ed i puntigli
Dalla testa mi cavò.

One fine day I met a fairy –
(You may think I am romancing) –
She drew near me, light and airy,
And with graceful step advancing
Threw me something rough and hairy,
Saying, "Take this gift and wear it.
You won't regret it!"
Then she disappeared in air, left me with an ass's skin.

Presso un picciolo abituro
Seco lei mi trasse un giorno;
E, togliendo giù dal muro
Del pacifico soggiorno
Una pelle di somaro:

"Prendi," disse, "o figlio caro!"

Poi disparve, e mi lasciò.

While I was lost in
Amazement and wonder,
A dreadful storm arose.
Thunder was crashing,
And like a waterfall
The rain was splashing
And lightning flashing.
I had no shelter,
Coat or umbrella,
Only the donkey's hide
Lay there nearby.
I slipped it over me,
It kept me dry.

Mentre ancor, tacito,
Guardo quel dono,
Il ciel s'annuvola,
Rimbomba il tuono,
Mista alla grandine
Scroscia la piova,
Scroscia la piova:
Ecco, le membra
Coprir mi giova
Col manto d'asino
Che mi donò.
Col manto d'asino
Che mi donò.

The sun came out again,
And I proceeded.
A horrid animal
Came out of nowhere.
Its eyes were gleaming,
Its chops were steaming,
I stood there petrified.
What could I do?

Finisce il turbine,
Lo fo due passi,
Che fiera orribile
Dianzi a me fassi:
Già già mi tocca,
L'ingorda bocca;
Già di difendermi
Speme non ho.

All of a sudden
The beast turned and bolted;
Smelling the donkey's hide
It was revolted.
It lost its appetite,
And ran away.

Ma il fiuto ignobile
Del mio vestito
Tolse alla belva
Si l'appetito,
Che, disprezzandomi,
Si rinselvò.

Take this advice, my friend,
And learn this lesson.
Scandal or calumny,
Injustice, dishonour,
Will never penetrate
A donkey's hide.

Cosi conoscere
Mi fe' la sorte
Ch'onte, pericoli,
Vergogna e morte
Col cuoio d'asino
Fuggir si può.

(Exeunt.)

Scene Eight. *Figaro alone. / No. 26. Recitative and aria*

FIGARO

Everything's ready; it must be
Time for their appointment. Did I hear
footsteps?
Susanna? Not a soul! Darkness infernal!

So I begin this evening
To learn the wretched trade
That it is to be a husband.
The traitress! To deceive me
On the day of our wedding.
I saw him read her letter, I saw him laugh
too,
Laughed myself, little knowing what I
laughed at.
Oh, Susanna, Susanna!
Have you brought me to this then?
Those eyes so sweet and candid,
And that face so ingenuous,
Who would not have believed them?
Oh, he who trusts a woman, fool, fool, and
fool again!

Tutto è disposto: l'ora
Dovrebbe esser vicina; io sento gente . . .
È dessa . . . non è alcun . . . Buia è la
notte . . .
Ed io comincio omai
A fare lo scimunito
Mestiero di marito . . .
Ingrata! nel momento
Della mia cerimonia . . .
Ei godeva leggendo: e nel vederlo

Io rideva di me senza saperlo.

Oh, Susanna! Susanna!
Quanta pena mi costi!
Con quell'ingenua faccia,
Con quegli occhi innocenti . . .
Chi creduto l'avria! . . .
Ah, che il fidarsi a donna è ognor follia!

Aria

Yes, fools you are and will be,   [41]
Fools till your eyes are opened,
Until you learn what women are,
And know them through and through.

Yes, you may call them angels,
But one day you'll awaken,
With faith that's rudely shaken,
To find it far from true.

They charm us with witchery
To waste us away,
Like tigers they fascinate,
To make us their prey,

They're meteors that dazzle us,
That dazzle us and blind us,
They're sirens who lure us on
Till on the rocks they find us.

You trust them for one day,
The next they deceive you,
They love you on Sunday,
On Monday they leave you.

For coaxing and crying,
Cajoling and cheating,
Intriguing and lying,
They cannot be beaten.
No mercy they show,
No, no, no, no!
The rest we'll pass over in silence,
What happens, you all of you know.

Aprite un po' quegli occhi
Uomini incauti e sciocchi,
Guardate queste femmine,
Guardate cosa son.

Queste chiamate Dee
Dagli ingannati sensi,
A cui tributa incensi
La debole ragion,

Son streghe che incantano
Per farci penar,
Sirene che cantano
Per farci affogar,

Civette che allettano
Per trarci le piume,
Comete che brillano
Per toglierci il lume;

Son rose spinose,
Son volpi vezzose,
Son orse benigne,
Colombe maligne,

Maestre d'inganni,
Amiche d'affanni
Che fingono, mentono,
Amore non senton,
Non senton pietà.
No, no, no, no!
Il resto nol dico,
Già ognuno lo sa.

(*He withdraws.*)

Scene Nine. *The Countess, Susanna and Marcellina; Figaro apart.*

Enter the Countess and Susanna dressed in each other's clothes and Marcellina / Recitative

SUSANNA

My lady, here's Marcellina
Says Figaro is coming.

Signora, ella mi disse
Che Figaro verravvi.

MARCELLINA

He's here already,   Anzi, è venuto:
So speak a little lower.   Abbassa un po' la voce.

SUSANNA

One lover listening, the other   Dunque, un ci ascolta, e l'altro
On the point of arriving!   Dèe venir a cercarmi.
We can begin.   Incominciam.

MARCELLINA

I'll hide within this arbour.   Io voglio qui celarmi.

(She goes into the same place as Barbarina.)

Scene Ten. *The Countess, Susanna and Figaro.*

SUSANNA

My lady, you are trembling; you feel it   Madama, voi tremate: avreste freddo?
cold here?

COUNTESS

The night is rather chilly; I shall go in now.   Parmi umida la notte . . . Io mi ritiro.

FIGARO
(aside)

Now we shall see the great dramatic   Eccoci della crisi al grande istante.
moment.

SUSANNA

I should prefer to stay here,   Io sotto queste piante,
If your ladyship will allow me,   Se Madama il permette,
And take the air a little among the pine   Resto a prendere il fresco una mezz'ora.
trees.

FIGARO
(aside)

The air – the pine trees!   Il fresco, il fresco!

COUNTESS

Yes, by all means do so.   Restaci, in buonora.
(She hides.)

SUSANNA
(aside)

That rascal Figaro's watching,   Il birbo è in sentinella
He shall have his reward.   Divertiamci anche noi:
I'll pay him out for daring to suspect me.   Diamogli la mercè de' dubbi suoi.
(aloud)

No. 27. Recitative and Aria

Now at last comes the moment   Giunse alfin il momento
When I yield, unresisting,   Che godrò senza affanno
To joy in his embraces. Why need I   In braccio all'idol mio! Timide cure,
tremble?
Away with silly scruples!   Uscite dal mio petto,
Shall they stand in the way of my desires?   A turbar non venite il mio diletto!
Here in this wood – 'twas made for lovers –   Oh, come par che all'amoroso foco
Everything breathes of rapture;   L'amenità del loco,
I feel it, 'tis all around me,   La terra e il ciel risponda!
While night enfolds us, our stolen joys   Come la notte i furti miei seconda!
concealing.

Aria

Then come, my heart's delight, no   [42]   Deh, vieni, non tardar, o gioia bella,
more delaying,
Come where awaits you love, and   Vieni ove amore per goder t'appella,
would be playing.

116

Not yet the moon on us her watch is keeping,
While in twilight veiled the world is sleeping.

I hear afar the ceaseless fountain sobbing;
Night winds whisper and set my pulses throbbing.

The grass is cool with flowers the senses exciting,
All to sweet delight of love inviting.

Come, let us hide us among these bowers of roses;
Come, my dearest! Sweetest of all is that flower that love uncloses.

Finchè non splende in ciel notturna face
Finchè l'aria è ancor bruna e il mondo tace.

Qui mormora il ruscel, qui scherza l'aura,
Che col dolce sussurro il cor ristaura;

Qui ridono i fioretti, e l'erba è fresca:

Ai piaceri d'amor qui tutto adesca.

Vieni, ben mio: tra queste piante ascose
Ti vo' la fronte incoronar di rose.

Scene Eleven. *The Countess, Figaro and Cherubino; then the Count. / Recitative*

FIGARO
(*aside*)

How shameless! Then all along She meant to deceive me! Am I awake or dreaming?

Perfida! e in quella forma Meco mentia? Non so s'io vegli o dorma.

CHERUBINO
(*entering humming*)

La la la, la la la, la lera.

[18] La la la, la la la, la lera.

COUNTESS
(*aside*)

That's Cherubino.

Il picciol paggio!

CHERUBINO

I heard a voice then; I'll go in and find Barbarina.

Io sento gente: entriamo Ove entrò Barbarina.

(*noticing the Countess*)

Ah, there I see a woman.

Oh, vedo qui una donna!

COUNTESS
(*aside*)

What shall I do now?

Ahi, me meschina!

CHERUBINO

That must be – no, I was wrong there – By the cloak I know it is Susanna.

M'inganno! A quel cappello Che nell'ombra vegg'io, parmi Susanna.

COUNTESS
(*aside*)

If my lord finds me now, then all is over!

E se il Conte ora vien? Sorte tiranna!

No. 28. Finale

CHERUBINO
[43]

Softly, softly I'll approach her, Waste of time that will not be.

Pian pianin le andrò più presso: Tempo perso non sarà.

COUNTESS
(*aside*)

Should my husband chance to find us, What a dreadful thing for me!

Ah, se il Conte arriva adesso, Qualche imbroglio accaderà!

CHERUBINO
(*to the Countess*)

Oh, Susanna!

Susannetta ...

Won't you answer?	Non risponde:
With her hand her face she's hiding;	Colla mano il volto asconde ...
Some adventure I shall see.	Or la burlo, in verità.

(He takes her hand and caresses it; the Countess tries to shake him off.)

COUNTESS
(altering her voice)

This is shameless, what presumption!	Arditello! sfacciatello!
I forbid you to come near.	Ite presto via di qua.

CHERUBINO

So coy then, just to tease me?	Smorfiosa, maliziosa,
I know why you're waiting here.	Io già so perchè sei qua.

COUNT
(peering at them, from a distance)

There she is, my own Susanna.	Ecco qui la mia Susanna.

FIGARO AND SUSANNA
(far apart from one another)

Here's the amorous pursuer!	Ecco qui l'uccellatore.

CHERUBINO
(still adressing the Countess)

Do not be so hard upon me!	Non far meco la tiranna!

SUSANNA, COUNT AND FIGARO
(aside)

Ah! How fast my heart is beating.	Ah, nel sen mi batte il core!
There's another man I see.	Un altr'uom con lei si sta.

COUNTESS
(sottovoce to Cherubino)

Go, or I will call assistance!	Via, partite, o chiamo gente.

CHERUBINO
(still holding her hand)

Won't you kiss me? What does it matter?	Dammi un bacio, o non fai niente.

SUSANNA, COUNT AND FIGARO
(aside)

By the voice 'tis Cherubino.	Alla voce, è quegli il paggio.

COUNTESS
(as before)

What impertinence! How dare you?	Anche un bacio! che coraggio!

CHERUBINO

Oh, but why should you refuse me	E perchè far io non posso
What my lord gets every day?	Quel che il Conte or or farà?

COUNTESS, SUSANNA, COUNT AND FIGARO
(all aside)

What presumption!	Temerario!

CHERUBINO

Why this denial? Oh why so prudish?	Oh ve' che smorfie!
You know what I saw today.	Sai ch'io fui dietro il sofà.

COUNTESS, SUSANNA, COUNT AND FIGARO
(still aside)

If he will not take refusal,	Se il ribaldo ancor sta saldo,
He will spoil our little play.	La faccenda guasterà.

CHERUBINO

Take a kiss then!	Prendi intanto ...

(The page tries to kiss the Countess; the Count gets between them and receives the kiss himself.)

COUNTESS AND CHERUBINO

Oh, heavens, his lordship! Oh, ciel! il Conte.

(The page goes after Barbarina.)

FIGARO
(aside)

I must see what's going on. Vo' veder cosa fan là.

COUNT

I will teach you better manners, Perchè voi nol ripetete,
So take that and then be gone! Ricevete questo qua.

(The Count tries to slap Cherubino; Figaro comes close up at that moment and receives the slap himself.)

FIGARO
(aside)

That's the way that I'm rewarded, Ah! ci ho fatto un bel guadagno,
I was rash to interfere! Ah! Colla mia curiosità!

COUNTESS AND COUNT
(Susanna hears the slap, and laughs.)

That's the way that he's rewarded, Ah! ci ha fatto un bel guadagno,
He was rash to interfere! Ah! Colla sua temerità.

SUSANNA

That's the way that he's rewarded, Ah! ci ha fatto un bel guadagno,
He was rash to interfere! Ah! Colla sua curiosità!

(Figaro retires.)

COUNT
(to the Countess)

Thank goodness, he's departed, Partito è alfin l'audace:
So let me talk to you. Accostati, ben mio!

COUNTESS

Indeed, my lord, I'm honoured, Giacchè così vi piace,
Say ... what you'd have me do. Eccomi qui, signor.

FIGARO
(aside)

A most obliging wife she is, Che compiacente femmina!
So faithful and so true! Che sposa di buon cor!

COUNT

Give me your hand, my angel. Porgimi la manina.

COUNTESS

My hand is yours. Io ve la dò.

COUNT

My dearest! Carina!

FIGARO

His dearest? Carino?

COUNT

This hand so soft and slender, Che dita tenerelle!
How delicate and tender! Che delicata pelle!
Oh, these enchanting fingertips Mi pizzica, mi stuzzica,
Set all my heart on fire! M'empie di un nuovo ardor.

SUSANNA, COUNTESS AND FIGARO

How blind his amorous passion, La cieca prevenzione

119

Deluding sense and reason,
With every false and vain desire!

Delude la ragione,
Inganna i sensi ognor.

COUNT

You have received a dowry,
But this too let me give you,
This diamond ring as token
Of my unending love.

Oltre la dote, o cara,
Ricevi anche un brillante,
Che a te porge un amante
In pegno del suo amor.

(He gives her a ring.)

COUNTESS

How can Susanna thank you?
Her gratitude how prove?

Tutto Susanna piglia
Dal suo benefattor.

SUSANNA, COUNT AND FIGARO
(aside)

Our
My } plot proceeds exactly,
The
Now faster it must move.

Va tutto a maraviglia!
Ma il meglio manca ancor.

COUNTESS
(to the Count)

Look there, my lord! I see the light
Of lanterns drawing near.

Signor, d'accese fiaccole
Io veggio il balenar.

COUNT

Come, hide my lovely Venus,
They will not find us here.
Then Venus now must hide her light,
They must not find us here.

Entriam, mia bella Venere.
Andiamoci a celar.
Entriam, mia bella Venere.
Andiamoci a celar.

SUSANNA AND FIGARO
(aside)

A lesson 'tis for husbands,
Who think they've naught to fear.

Mariti scimuniti,
Venite ad imparar.

COUNTESS

I think it's rather dark there.

Al buio, signor mio?

COUNT

That suits me very well, dear.
You know it's not to read a book
I want to go in there!

È quello che vogl'io:
Tu sai che là per leggere
Io non desio d'entrar.

FIGARO
(aside)

The wretch is going there with him.
She's faithless, that is clear.

La perfida lo seguita:
È vano il dubitar.

COUNTESS AND SUSANNA

Now both our men are in the trap,
We've caught them, that is clear.

I furbi sono in trappola,
Cammina ben l'affar.

(Figaro crosses the stage.)

COUNT
(disguising his voice)

Who's that there?

Chi passa?

FIGARO
(enraged)

No-one special.

Passa gente!

COUNTESS
(sottovoce to the Count)

That's Figaro. I'm off.

È Figaro: men vò.

Yes, yes, that's safer; I'll join you soon.   Andate: io poi verrò.

(*The Count disappears amongst the bushes, whilst the Countess goes into the arbour on the right.*)

FIGARO

Silence and peace are all around,	Tutto è tranquillo e placido:
The lovely Venus hides her light,	Entrò la bella Venere.
With Mars conjoined in love's embrace.	Col vago Marte prendere
Vulcan's the part for me to play,	Nuovo Vulcan del secolo,
And catch them in my net.	In rete la potrò.

SUSANNA
(*disguising her voice*)

Oh Figaro! Speak softly!   Ehi, Figaro, tacete!

FIGARO

Aha! There's the Countess!	Oh, questa è la Contessa ...

(*to Susanna*)

You're just in time, my lady,	A tempo qui giungete ...
You're just in time to catch them.	Vedrete là voi stessa ...
His lordship is with Susanna;	Il Conte e la mia sposa ...
Your ladyship shall see them,	Di propria man la cosa
For now the trap is set.	Toccar io vi farò.

SUSANNA
(*forgetting to disguise her voice*)

You needn't speak so loudly,	Parlate un po' più basso.
I need no explanation,	Di qua non muovo passo,
And vengeance I'll have too.	Ma vendicar mi vo'.

FIGARO
(*aside*)

Susanna!   Susanna!

(*to Susanna*)

You said vengeance?   Vendicarsi?

SUSANNA

Yes!   Sì.

FIGARO

Vengeance? What need have you of vengeance?	Come, come, potria farsi?

(*aside*)

She means to set a trap for me,	La volpe vuol sorprendermi,
I'll help her do it too,	E secondar la vo',
I see what she will do.	E secondar la vo'.

SUSANNA
(*aside*)

I mean to set a trap for him,	L'iniquo io vo' sorprendere;
And this is what I'll do.	Poi so quel che farò.

FIGARO
(*in comic, affected tones*)

Ah, if my lady desires,	Ah, se Madama il vuole!
Ah, my lady!	Ah madama!

SUSANNA
(*aside*)

I see he's all too ready.	Su, via, manco parole,
So now we'll have a love-scene.	Su, via, manco parole.

FIGARO
(*as before*)

Here, at your feet, my lady,	Eccomi ai vostri piedi ...
I burn with warm emotion,	Ho pieno il cor di fuoco.

Accept my adoration,
Think how you were betrayed!

Esaminate il loco . . .
Pensate al traditor.

SUSANNA
(*aside*)

Now is the time to punish him,
I long to box his ears.
I burn with rage and fury.

Come la man mi pizzica!
Che smania! che furor!
Che smania! che furor!

FIGARO
(*aside*)

Oh, how my bosom swells with love!
Her fury calms my fears.
I love to see her rage and fury.

Come il polmon mi si altera!
Che smania! che calor!
Che smania! che calor!

SUSANNA
(*altering her voice slightly*)

No more than adoration?

E senza alcun affetto? . . .

FIGARO

To speak my heart I dared not.
But now the words are spoken.
Give me your hand in token –

Suppliscavi il dispetto.
Non perdiam tempo invano,
Datemi un po' la mano . . .

SUSANNA
(*giving him a slap, using her natural voice*)

So take it, and take that!

Servitevi, signor!

FIGARO

You hit me!

Che schiaffo!

SUSANNA

Take that, Sir, and that, Sir,
And that will teach you, you rascal,
and that will teach you –

E questo, e questo
E ancora questo, e questo, e
poi questo' altro!

(*slapping him in time*)

FIGARO

Have mercy, I beseech you!

Non batter cosi presto.

SUSANNA
(*still slapping him*)

You rascal, that will teach you
A lesson that you will not forget.

E questo, signor scaltro,
E questo, e poi questo'altro ancor!

FIGARO

Oh gorgeous blows so passionate!
Oh blissful sign of love!

Oh, schiaffi graziosissimi!
Oh, mio felice amor!

SUSANNA

You dare to go philandering,
And that's what you will get!
Be false and go philandering,
And that's what you will get:

Impara, impara, o perfido,
A fare il seduttor.
Impara, impara, o perfido,
A fare il seduttor.

FIGARO
(*falling on his knees*)

Now Susanna, be kind and forgive me;
All in vain did you try to deceive me;
Why your voice told me plainly 'twas you.

[44] Pace, pace, mio dolce tesoro:
Io conobbi la voce che adoro,
E che impressa ognor serbo nel cor.

SUSANNA
(*smiling in surprise*)

Then you knew me?

La mia voce?

FIGARO

Your voice told me plainly.

La voce che adoro.

122

Then, my dearest be kind and forgive me,	Pace, pace, mio dolce tesoro,
Doubt no longer your lover was true.	Pace, pace, mio tenero amor.

COUNT
(aside, returning)

Where's Susanna? I wish I could find her.	Non la trovo, e girai tutto il bosco.

SUSANNA AND FIGARO

That's the voice of { my / your } noble pursuer.	Questi è il Conte, alla voce il conosco.

COUNT
(in the direction of the arbour which the Countess entered)

Oh, Susanna! Where are you? I'm seeking.	Ehi, Susanna . . . sei sorda . . . sei muta?

SUSANNA
(sottovoce to Figaro)

He knows little with whom he was speaking.	Bella! bella! non l'ha conosciuta!

FIGARO
(sottovoce to Susanna)

Whom?	Chi?

SUSANNA
(as before)

My lady.	Madama.

FIGARO
(as before)

My lady?	Madama?

SUSANNA
(as before)

My lady!	Madama.

SUSANNA AND FIGARO
(sottovoce)

Well, 'tis time for our play to be ending;	La commedia, idol mio, terminiamo:
Let's console this poor lover at last.	Consoliamo il bizzarro amator.

FIGARO
(disguising his voice, and throwing himself at Susanna's feet)

Noble lady, be mine, I adore you!	Si, Madama, voi siete il ben mio.

COUNT
(aside)

'Tis my wife there, after all she is guilty.	La mia sposa! Ah, senz'arme son io!

FIGARO
(still kneeling)

Oh, be gracious and grant me your favour.	Un ristoro al mio cor concedete.

SUSANNA
(disguising her voice)

I am yours, and I'll wait on your pleasure.	Io son qui, faccio quel che volete.

COUNT
(aside)

Oh, the traitors!	Ah, ribaldi!

SUSANNA AND FIGARO

Let us hasten where pleasure invites us,	Ah, corriamo, mio bene,
To make up for the pains of the past.	E le pene compensi il piacer.

(Figaro rises, and they both go off to the arbour left.)

Scene Twelve. *The Count, Countess, Susanna, Figaro, Marcellina, Bartolo, Cherubino, Barbarina, Antonio, Basilio, Don Curzio, Servants.*

COUNT
(stopping Figaro)

Ho, you men, there! Ho! Bring lights here!   Gente, gente! All'armi, all'armi!

(Susanna goes into the arbour.)

FIGARO
(pretending to be terrified)

'Tis his lordship!   Il padrone!

COUNT

Help me, help me, come this way now!   Gente, gente, aiuto, aiuto!

FIGARO
(as before)

I am ruined!   Son perduto!

(Antonio, Basilio, Bartolo, Don Curzio and servants with lighted torches run in.)

BASILIO, DON CURZIO, ANTONIO AND BARTOLO

What has happened?   Cosa avvenne?

COUNT

        See. Here's a villain   Il scellerato!
Has insulted and betrayed me,   M'ha tradito, m'ha infamato!
And with whom you soon shall see.   E con chi, state a veder.

BASILIO, DON CURZIO, ANTONIO AND BARTOLO
(aside)

I'm astounded, quite confounded,   Son stordito, sbalordito.
Surely true this cannot be.   Non mi par che ciò sia ver.

FIGARO

They're astounded, quite confounded,   Son storditi, sbalorditi:
Oh, what joy this is to me!   Oh, che scena, che piacer!

COUNT

In vain is resistance,   Invan resistete,
Come forth now, my lady,   Uscite, Madama!
Receive the reward of   Il premio or avrete
Your virtuous career.   Di vostra onestà.
Cherubino!   Il paggio!

(The Count pulls Cherubino by the arm; the latter struggles not to come out, and can only be half seen. After the page come Barbarina, Marcellina and Susanna, dressed in the Countess's clothes. She holds her handkerchief over her face and kneels at the Count's feet.)

ANTONIO

     My daughter!   Mia figlia!

FIGARO

My mother!   Mia madre!

BASILIO, DON CURZIO, ANTONIO, BARTOLO AND FIGARO

    The Countess!   Madama!

COUNT

The plot is discovered,   Scoperta è la trama,
The traitress is here!   La perfida è qua.

(They all kneel down, one by one.)

SUSANNA

Forgive me, forgive me!   Perdono, perdono!

COUNT

No, no, I renounce you.   No, no, non sperarlo!

FIGARO

Forgive her, forgive her!	Perdono, perdono!

COUNT

No, no, I'll denounce you!	No, no, non vo' darlo!

SUSANNA, CHERUBINO, BARBARINA, MARCELLINA, BASILIO, DON CURZIO, ANTONIO, BARTOLO AND FIGARO

Forgive her, forgive her!	Perdono, perdono!

COUNT
(louder)

No, no, no, no, no!	No, no, no, no, no!

COUNTESS
(coming out of the arbour)

May I then for pardon	Almeno io per loro
At last intercede?	Perdono otterrò.

(She tries to kneel but the Count prevents her.)

COUNT, BASILIO, DON CURZIO, ANTONIO AND BARTOLO

Oh Heavens! The Countess!	Oh cielo! che veggio!
What a vision deludes me?	Deliro! vaneggio!
Or do I behold her indeed?	Che creder non so.

COUNT
(entreating her)

My lady, forgive me.	Contessa, perdono.

COUNTESS

Once more I forgive you,	Più docile io sono,
I cannot refuse.	E dico di si.

ALL

Let all learn the lesson,	Ah! tutti contenti
Forget and forgive,	Saremo cosi.
Whoever contented	Ah! tutti contenti
And happy would live.	Saremo cosi.

Let this day of storm and tempest,	Questo giorno di tormenti,
Day of sorrow, day of madness,	Di capricci e di follia,
Now give way to joy and gladness,	In contenti e in allegria
And to love and gay delight.	Solo amor può terminar.

Good friends and lovers, your pleasure be taking,	Sposi, amici, al ballo! al gioco!
All the echoes to the noise of laughter waking.	Alle mine date fuoco,
To the sound of merry music	Ed al suon di lieta marcia
We will revel all the night.	Corriam tutti a festeggiar.

Finis.

Discography The specialist is referred to *Opera on Record* (ed. Alan Blyth, Hutchinson 1979) for detailed analysis and comment. The following is a selective list of complete recordings, all in stereo and sung in Italian.

Conductor	*Boehm*	*Karajan*	*Solti*
Company/Orchestra	**Deutsche Oper, Berlin**	**Vienna PO**	**London PO**
Date	*1967*	*1979*	*1984*
Count	D. Fischer-Dieskau	T. Krause	T. Allen
Figaro	H. Prey	J. van Dam	S. Ramey
Susanna	E. Mathis	I. Cotrubas	L. Popp
Countess	G. Janowitz	A. Tomowa-Sintow	K. te Kanawa
Cherubino	T. Troyanos	F. von Stade	F. von Stade
UK LP Number	–	–	–
UK Tape Number	–	–	–
UK CD Number	DG 415 520-2GH3 (3)	Decca 421 125-2DH3 (3)	Decca 410 150-2DH3 (3)
US LP Number	–	–	–
US Tape Number	–	–	–
US CD Number	DG 415 520-GH3 (3)	Decca 421 125-2LH3 (3)	Decca 410 150-2LH3 (3)

Conductor	Marriner	Muti	Haitink	Ostman
Company/Orchestra	Academy of St Martin-in-the-Fields	Vienna PO	London PO	Drottningholm Court Theatre
Date	1987	1987	1988	1988
Count	R. Raimondi	J. Hynninen	R. Stillwell	H. Hågegard
Figaro	J. van Dam	T. Allen	C. Desderi	P. Salomaa
Susanna	B. Hendricks	K. Battle	G. Rolandi	B. Bonney
Countess	L. Popp	M. Price	F. Lott	A. Auger
Cherubino	A. Baltsa	A. Murray	F. Esham	A. Nafé
UK LP Number	Philips 416 370-1PH3 (3)	EMI EX 270576-3 (3)	EMI EX 749753-1 (3)	L'Oiseau-Lyre 421 333-10H3 (3)
UK Tape Number	Philips 416 370-4PH3 (3)	EMI EX 270576-5 (3)	EMI EX 749753-4 (3)	L'Oiseau-Lyre 421 333-40H3 (3)
UK CD Number	Philips 416 370-2PH3 (3)	EMI CDS 747978-8 (3)	EMI CDS 749753-2 (3)	L'Oiseau-Lyre 421 333-20H3 (3)
US LP Number	Philips 416 370-1PH3 (3)	EMI EX 270576-3 (3)	EMI EX 749753-1 (3)	L'Oiseau-Lyre 421 333-10H3 (3)
US Tape Number	Philips 416 370-4PH3 (3)	EMI EX 270576-5 (3)	EMI EX 749753-4 (3)	L'Oiseau-Lyre 421 333-40H3 (3)
US CD Number	Philips 416 370-2PH3 (3)	EMI CDS 747978-8 (3)	EMI CDS 749753-2 (3)	L'Oiseau-Lyre 421 333-20H3 (3)

Bibliography

Alfred Einstein's *Mozart, his Character, his Work* (London, 1969), which has an illuminating passage on the opera in the context of Mozart's whole output, contains a surprising quantity of detailed observation for so short and readable a text. *Three Mozart Operas* by R.B. Moberly (London, 1967) and *The Operas of Mozart* by William Mann (London, paperback, 1988) each study the opera in depth. Yet E.J. Dent's *Mozart Operas: A Critical Study* (London, 1913, 1947), the first major study of them in English, still makes an excellent introduction combining as it does scholarship and wit.

Readers interested in the autograph score may consult 'Mozart's Manuscripts in Florence', *Music and Letters* (Vol. 40, no. 4, Oct. 1959) by Michael and Christopher Raeburn. This article discusses the earliest known copy of Mozart's 1789 revisions of *Figaro* including the discovery by the authors of the revised Count's aria.

There are revised editions of two stimulating commentaries on Mozart's operas: Joseph Kerman's *Opera as Drama* (Faber, 1988) and Brigid Brophy's *Mozart the Dramatist* (London, 1988).

Emily Anderson's translation of *The Letters of Mozart and his Family* (3 vols, London, 1938) vividly fills in the background to the composition.

The best English biography of da Ponte is by April FitzLyon *Lorenzo da Ponte* (London, 1982). His *Memorie*, translated by Elisabeth Abbott (Philadelphia, 1929) make fascinating reading. The passage in Patrick J. Smith's *The Tenth Muse: A Historical Study of the Opera Libretto* (London, 1971) is the best survey of contemporary librettos. A fascinating study of the composer by Wolfgang Hildesheimer is *Mozart* (paperback, London, 1988) and Andrew Steptoe's new survey of *Mozart-da Ponte (a cultural and musical background)* is published by Oxford, 1989.

The plays of Beaumarchais, translated by John Wood, are available in Penguin (1962, reprinted 1979) and there is a biography by Cynthia Cox, *The Real Figaro* (Longmans, 1962).

Contributors

John Wells, author, playwright and translator of librettos, has translated both the *Barber of Seville* and *The Marriage of Figaro*.

Basil Deane is Professor of Music at the Barber Institute of Fine Arts at the University of Birmingham.

Stephen Oliver is the composer of numerous operas, including *Mario and the Magician*, and much incidental music for theatre and television. He has been commissioned to write an opera for ENO.